PORSCHE
911 TURBO

Osprey AutoHistory

PORSCHE 911 TURBO

3 and 3.3 litre; Project no. 930

MICHAEL COTTON

Published in 1981 by Osprey Publishing Limited,
12–14 Long Acre, London WC2 9LP
Member company of the George Philip Group

First reprint Spring 1982
Second reprint Spring 1984

United States distribution by

Osceola, Wisconsin 54020, USA

British Library Cataloguing in Publication Data

Cotton, Michael
    Porsche 911 turbo.—(Autohistory)
    1. Porsche automobile—History
    I. Title
    629.2′222   TL215.P75

ISBN 0-85045-400-X

Editor Tim Parker
Associate Michael Sedgwick
Photography Mirco Decet
Design Fred Price

Filmset in Great Britain
Printed in Spain by Grijelmo S.A., Bilbao

Contents

Introduction
6

Chapter 1 **The background story**
12

Chapter 2 **Evolution**
23

Chapter 3 **The first road car**
33

Chapter 4 **The racers**
51

Chapter 5 **On the road**
63

Chapter 6 **3.3-litres**
86

Chapter 7 **The specials**
98

Chapter 8 **What the road testers said**
108

Specifications
130

Production schedules
132

Acknowledgements
133

Index
134

Introduction

Any motor manufacturer with spirit will strive to produce a top model capable of proving its worth in competitions, earning all-important publicity and a reputation which will reflect well on other products in the range. Only occasionally does such a machine achieve real greatness, and among these the Porsche 911 Turbo is arguably the most renowned.

How can anyone measure the absolute greatness of a car? In terms of outright speed and acceleration the engineers are progressing all the time, so one cannot compare the reputation of a Ferrari Daytona or a Porsche Turbo with, for instance, a Bentley $4\frac{1}{2}$ or a Jaguar D type. Superiority over contemporaries is a useful measure; monetary value among collectors is another, though value depends very much on the quantity available. As it happens there is no shortage of Porsche Turbos on the British market at £28,000 (1981 values) at a time when a Ford GT40 might fetch anything up to £70,000. But few more than 100 GT40s were ever built, whereas in the six years from autumn 1974 to autumn 1980 no fewer than 7348 Porsche Turbos were produced in the Stuttgart-Zuffenhausen factory, including 96 racing cars of the types 934 (Group 4) and 935 (Group 5). It may not be until the turn of the century that motoring historians will judge the greatness of the Porsche Turbo, but it's fair to say that already its place among the supercars of the 20th Century is assured.

What makes a Porsche Turbo so special?

Anyone who has driven one can tell straight away that it's like driving a racing car on the road. *Autocar*'s first road report in April 1975 summed up: 'It may look like an ordinary 911 but the effect is shattering.' The American magazine *Car & Driver* said succinctly: 'Super Turbo: the people's racer—only professional drivers with up-to-date medical certificates and fresh advanced training slips from the Bondurant school need apply'. But just in case the writer gave the impression that the Turbo is a fierce, intractable motor car, he added: 'If you possess priestly restraint you might go four miles in the Turbo before you stomp on the gas pedal with both feet and let the mighty torque curve ratchet you back a few notches in the seat'.

That's a very important point, because *all* Porsches, even the out-and-out racing cars, are capable of being driven quietly. Professor Dr. Ernst Fuhrmann, chairman of Porsche's executive board for eight years, said in an interview with *Motor*: 'I always have good cars from my company with high performance, but my wife is an average driver yet she can get in the car and drive it. I drove the first 911 Turbo for two years before it was on sale, but my wife didn't know anything about that. She jumped in the car and drove it. That is the Porsche philosophy: every young girl and every engineer can drive the car. That's the way it should be.'

Some people refer to the car as 'the Porsche Turbo'. Today of course we also have the 924 Turbo, and the marketing men began referring to the original model, correctly, as 'the 911 Turbo'. The engineers at Weissach still call it 'the 930' because the turbocharged development of the 911 was in fact project number 930 on the drawing boards. (The 924 Turbo is project number 931, but the 2-litre car is never referred to as 931 outside the research and development centre). So through-

Professor Dr. Ernst Fuhrmann, chairman of Porsche from 1972 to 1980

out this book the car will be referred to as the 911 Turbo.

When it was first announced at the Paris Show in October 1974, the 911 Turbo had a quoted horsepower rating of 260 DIN from its flat-six cylinder, all alloy, air-cooled engine boosted by a KKK exhaust driven turbocharger. At the time the 3-litre Carrera RSR, intended for racing, was going out of production, together with its mechanically injected but normally aspirated engine producing 230 horsepower. For normal road purposes the 911 Turbo topped a production range consisting of the 2.7-litre 911 (150 bhp), the 911S (175 bhp) and the 911 SC Carrera (210 bhp). With a top speed of 155 mph and standstill to 100 mph acceleration in the order of 13 seconds, the 911 Turbo was indeed the brightest jewel in Porsche's crown.

In fact though, the Turbo was not conceived so much as the ultimate road car as the basis for a family of production-based racing cars intended for the World Championship for Makes, which would be run to new regulations in 1976. The regulations would demand that a minimum of 400 of the basic type to be raced must be built within two years, though of course the modifications that could be carried out for racing purposes were almost infinite. The new formula was dubbed 'silhouette' because so long as the car looked similar to its production ancestor and so long as it had basically the same power unit in the same position, it could be developed into a real racing car without offending the rule-makers. And indeed it was. Before the 935 derivative reached the end of its development it was producing no less than 750 horsepower, 50 per cent more than a contemporary Grand Prix car!

The story goes that the engineers planned that 400 cars would be made and sold and that would be

the end of the matter. Doctor Ernst Fuhrmann had other ideas and decreed that no matter how expensive the car might turn out to be, it should be fully equipped with air conditioning, stereo radio, electrically operated windows, leather upholstery and trim, tinted glass, heated front and rear windows and deep pile carpet: it should in other words be the flagship of the range, the last word in performance with comfort. Bear in mind that previous production cars intended for racing, such as the 911 Carrera RS, had been partially stripped out, lightened and even had some of their soundproofing omitted, and you can see what a reversal of policy Dr. Fuhrmann was dictating. But he was absolutely right, because the Turbo would indeed become the supercar of the 1970s and give the Porsche company a public image that couldn't have been matched even by the Carrera 3 and the 3-litre 911 SC. They too could exceed 140 mph comfortably, but they lacked the enormous punch of a jet fighter on the runway that set the Turbo apart from anything else on the public highway.

Old and new at Works 2. On the right, the factory buildings where 911 and 928 models are built. On the left, the extension to the 928 line just opened, also housing the well appointed Casino restaurants for the 4000 employees

9

The 3-litre Carrera, from which the 911 Turbo was developed, also showing some of the more vital components including fabricated steel rear suspension trailing arms

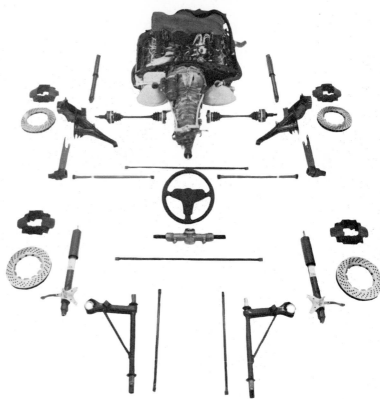

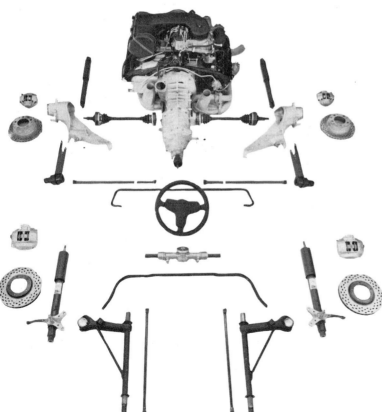

The 911 Turbo, clearly showing its ancestry to the Carrera. Suspension trailing arms are now cast in alloy and the brake system is entirely different (though the cross-drilled brakes were postponed for three years)

11

Chapter 1
The background story

Turbocharging is a form of supercharging, which is a means of increasing the amount of charge (ie fuel/air mixture) which can be induced into the cylinder before the compression stroke, thus increasing the power. But whereas a supercharger is normally mechanically driven, off the crankshaft or camshaft, the turbocharger is built into the exhaust system and therefore uses a source of energy that would otherwise be entirely wasted. There is of course some back-pressure which reduces efficiency, but it is negligible in contrast with the available increase in power.

The principle of turbocharging has been known for over 75 years. In 1905 a Swiss engineer, Alfred Büchi, was granted a patent for a four-stroke engine equipped with a compressor on the intake side and a turbine on the exhaust side. Ten years later Büchi was granted another patent for a form of turbocharging that is favoured today, with the tandem compressor driven by the exhaust gases. In the 1920s the turbocharger was developed for marine purposes, and by the late 1930s Professor Porsche's design team in Stuttgart was experimenting with turbocharging on the Volkswagen . . . but they were defeated by the low speed of the exhaust gases! Turbocharging was successfully applied to fighter aircraft during the war and further developed in truck engines in the post-war years.

As early as 1952 the first turbocharged diesel racing car made its appearance at Indianapolis. Another decade passed before turbocharging became anything like popular in the Offenhauser and Meyer-Drake engined cars at Indy, but that was the start of the trend. These early turbo racing cars were badly afflicted by throttle lag, and were therefore only really suitable for the very high-speed tracks like Indy; the engines would have been hopeless on a Grand Prix circuit without further development. By the same token supercharging with its more immediate response, was still favoured by a few manufacturers for racing cars, for the same reason. The problem with turbochargers was (and to a small extent still is) that while the car is slowing down the turbine in the exhaust system also slows down from its normal 100,000 rpm and does not respond readily when the accelerator is depressed again. Sophisticated by-pass valves have virtually overcome the problem today, to the point where the driver of a road car wouldn't notice any throttle lag, and Grand Prix drivers can live with it without qualm.

Porsche started work on turbocharger development in 1970, the year the FIA (motor racing's ruling body) announced that, from 1972 it would change the sportscar formula to banish the flat-12 Porsche 917 which was to win two World Championships with consummate ease. The Stuttgart factory had its eyes on the Canadian-American Championship (Can-Am) for unlimited capacity sports-racing cars, just the sort of arena that any manufacturer selling half its produce to America would be interested in! Jo Siffert had driven Porsche's first Can-Am cars with some success in 1969, first with the 917 PA which was effectively a spider version of the type 917 World Championship car. The factory didn't compete in the States until August 1971 when Siffert drove a normally aspirated 917/10 5-litre car in the first of four races that season.

During 1971 Porsche's engineers Hans Mezger and Valentine Schaeffer developed a 4.5-litre flat-12 type 917 engine fitted with twin Eberspächer turbocharger units which turned at 90,000 rpm. The compression ratio was reduced from 10.5:1 to just 6.5:1, the speed of the gear-driven cooling fan was increased to raise the volume of air passing over the cylinders, the exhaust valve stems were chrome plated to overcome problems with the guides, and the oil supply was improved. Mezger notes that at full throttle the exhaust gas temperature was 1000 to 1100 degrees centigrade, which gives some idea of the enormity of the problems which had to be tackled in the turbocharger area.

With a boost pressure of around 1.3 bar (18.5 psi) the power output of the 4.5-litre motor

Founding father of the 911 series, Ferry Porsche. Here, opening Porsche Cars' Great Britain new Reading HQ

Far right Ing. Hans Mezger, head of advanced engine developments

was raised from 580 horsepower to some 850 horsepower at 8000 rpm. At first the test drivers complained after runs at Weissach and Hockenheim that the prototype had poor throttle response and this became the main area of development. The virtual answer was the introduction of pressure relief butterfly valves placed between the inlet manifolds and the inlet valves. Connected with the throttle valves by a linkage, the valves opened when the throttles were shut off completely thus dropping the intake manifold pressure immediately.

This had the effect of relieving back-pressure on the turbocharger and keeping the turbine speed up to an acceptable level for the few seconds that the throttle might be closed. This also had

Two World Championship victories fell to Porsche in 1973, both unexpected and at opposite ends of the speed scale. In January Peter Gregg/Hurley Haywood won the Daytona 24 Hours (shown here), and in May Herbert Mueller/Gijs van Lennep the last Targa Florio at the wheel of the factory prototype

The result of all the development work was a 260 horsepower car that captured the imagination of Porsche's wealthy clientele—the Turbo. Not at the debut Paris Show but at Birmingham in 1978

the desired effect of improving the engine's braking effect, since no boost would pass the throttles. Also, shocks and vibrations in the pressure line were avoided, reducing wear and tear on the turbocharger.

Another useful development was the wastegate valve. Operated by a diaphragm, this valve located between the exhaust manifold and the turbine, opened when the boost had reached the required level. In early developments the wastegate blow-off pressure was controlled by a screw, but by 1973 Mark Donohue was entrusted with a control knob inside the car which could be used to increase or decrease the boost pressure—and for every increase of 0.1 bar (1.4 psi) the power output rose by 50 bhp!

All the research was transferred to the 5-litre flat-12 engine for the 1972 racing season, when Roger Penske ran a pair of 917/10 models with no less than 1000 horsepower for Mark Donohue and George Follmer. The Penske team literally swept the previously dominant McLaren team aside, winning six races and giving Follmer the Can-Am title for the year.

For the 1973 season the factory engines were further developed and Donohue was equipped with the 917/30 which, among other things, now had a 5.4-litre engine in turbocharged state producing a massive 1100 horsepower. This is by far the most powerful engine ever made for road racing purposes, enabling the 917 to accelerate from a standstill to 100 km/h (62 mph) in 2.3

In 1972 the Can-Am scene was overtaken by the 917/10 models of George Follmer and Mark Donohue. The turbocharged 12-cylinder cars trounced the previously dominant McLarens, and Follmer captured the title

17

seconds, and to 200 km/h in approximately 5.3 seconds. With this car Donohue set a closed-circuit speed record of 221.12 mph at Talladega in 1974.

With Porsche dominating the North American scene, the organisers had a big re-think in the wake of the 1973 oil crisis and changed the rules so effectively in 1974 (at very short notice) that the turbocharged Porsches became quite uncompetitive, and it was at that point that the Germans decided to try another line of development: the turbocharging of the 911 Carrera.

The Carrera was announced late in 1972 with competitions uppermost in mind, though more than 1000 cars were sold for road use. The RSR racing version, with a 2.8-litre engine tuned up to 308 horsepower, was ideal for Group 4 racing and even won two World Championship races in Prototype form in 1973: the Daytona 24-Hours (Peter Gregg/Hurley Haywood) and the Targa Florio (Gijs van Lennep/Herbert Müller). Despite these successes, though, it couldn't be regarded as a true challenger to the Matra, Gulf-Mirage, Ferrari and Alfa Romeo T33 prototype sports cars with their 450 bhp-plus Grand Prix engines, so the Porsche factory embarked on a turbocharged version of the Carrera for endurance racing.

A good deal of experience could be transferred from the flat-12 to the production flat-6 engine, but one major change had to be carried out. Under the FIA's rules, supercharged and turbocharged cars have their swept capacity multiplied by 1.4, and since the maximum engine capacity for prototype cars was 3000 cc it followed that the Porsche turbo engine could have a swept volume of no more than 2142 cc.

The original 2-litre 911 alloy block was adopted for the new engine, retaining the 66 mm stroke while the bores in the Nikasil cylinders were

taken out to 83 mm, giving a swept capacity of exactly 2142 cc. Surprisingly the standard crankshaft could be used without modifications, though titanium con-rods from the Carrera 6 were fitted. The pistons were new, of course, and the compression ratio was reduced to 6.5:1.

A single turbocharger made by KKK was installed, this sufficing to boost what was, after all, akin to a half-size 917 engine, and a Garrett boost pressure by-pass valve adopted. Twin-plug heads similar to those on the 2.34 and 2.5-litre

The Porsche Carrera RSR 2.1-litre turbo ran well through the 1974 season with Martini sponsorship, its best result being second overall at Le Mans

Understeer is the predominant handling characteristic of the 911 Turbo at all normal speeds, switching to oversteer only in the final stages of adhesion

racing engines were chosen, though with the exhaust valves enlarged and sodium cooled valves were used on the inlet and exhaust sides, made of titanium (inlet) and Nimonic (exhaust). With a boost pressure of 1.3 to 1.4 bar (18.5 to 20 psi) the output was rated at between 490 and 516 horse-power at 7600 rpm.

Whilst certainly the equal in power of the Formula 1 engined prototypes it would meet on the circuits, the Porsche Turbo-Carrera was by comparison massively proportioned and a good deal heavier. The standard steel body was retained but, in common with the 1973 Carrera prototype, the 1974 Turbo had its front and rear lids, doors, front wheel arches and fenders made of thin fibreglass. The fuel tank was moved from the front compartment to within the car, in the rear seat area, enabling the designers to reduce weight at the front.

Modifications at the rear were even more far-reaching as an aluminium space-frame was installed to carry the engine and rear suspension, the springing now being by means of titanium coil springs instead of steel torsion bars. One way and another the total weight was pared down to 825 kilogrammes, 250 lighter than a roadgoing Carrera RS. Even so, the Turbo-Carrera was still 175 kg above the minimum weight for the class, and the only consolation was that none of the prototype teams could get down to the 650 kg limit either—700 kg was about the mark, possibly 725 kg in Le Mans trim.

There was little chance of outright success in the field of racing—unless Porsche 'got lucky' and the prototypes proved frail—but the factory decided to run a pair of Turbo-Carreras in 1974 in order to develop them fully, perhaps pick up a good placing at Le Mans ... and above all, to prepare for the new 'silhouette formula' which was in prospect (though not confirmed) for 1976.

After extensive testing at the Ricard circuit in southern France, the Turbo-Carrera made its debut at the Le Mans trials and 4-hour race in March. It was a rather untypical Porsche outing as a multitude of problems afflicted the team throughout the weekend, the cars suffering from high oil temperatures, strained transmissions and eventually stopping with over-revved engines.

Turbocharging basically standard engines was not, in itself, causing mechanical failures but was overheating the pistons, valves and cylinder heads and the standard type 915 5-speed gearbox was not considered to be up to the task of transmitting 500 horsepower and over 400 lb. ft torque. Nevertheless a standard sized 225 mm clutch was successfully retained, with sintered linings.

A major modification before the cars' next appearance at Monza involved fitting an air-to-air intercooler, which lowered the temperature of the incoming compressed air from 150 degrees to approximately 75 degrees centigrade. From then on the Porsche factory entries were normally reliable, and scored a useful number of points in the World Championship.

The highlight of the season, as usual, was the 24-hour race at Le Mans where the factory entered a single Turbo-Carrera. As the race wore on it moved up the leader board, until, at the 18-hour mark, it was lying second to a Matra which was stranded in the pits having its gearbox rebuilt. The Porsche was only a lap in arrears when the French car restarted, but any hopes the Germans might have held were dashed when the Porsche's fifth gear broke and the car had to run the remainder of the race without the most important ratio in the box. Even so, it did cruise home in second place at the finish, a particularly worthy result for a production car, and at the season's end Porsche had amassed enough points to claim third place in the World Championship table.

Porsche now had a wealth of experience with turbocharging to concentrate on two areas of development: the 911 Turbo road car announced in September 1974, and the future racing regulations to come into effect in January 1976.

Chapter 2
Evolution

Porsche, with 4000 employees involved in production and another 1000 in research and development, has a relatively short chain of command, each manager having his clearly defined responsibilities. In overall control of the company is Dr. Ferry Porsche, chairman of the supervisory board and head of the ten family shareholders. To him and his board falls the final decision in matters of important policy. Professor Dr. Ernst Fuhrmann, a former Porsche engineer and designer of the original 356 Carrera twin-cam power unit, was chairman of the executive board from 1972 until 1980 and had the last word on any matters that didn't concern the general longterm future of the company. Reporting to him was Dipl. Ing. Helmuth Bott, director of engineering and the man in control of the Weissach research and development centre.

Each major project has a 'father'—a man who takes overall command of the undertaking and ensures that his designers communicate properly and receive all the assistance, materials, research facilities and back-up they need. Not least, he has to control the project's budget, which tends to overrun when engineers are engaged in research and development. Helmuth Flegl, a young man with the impeccable credential of having supervised the Can-Am dominance of Porsche in 1972/73, was made father of the 911 Turbo project. Reporting to Flegl were Wolfgang Berger, the

Right *Dipl. Ing. Helmuth Bott, director of engineering*

Far right *Wolfgang Berger, project leader for the 911 Turbo development*

project leader, and engineers Reitter (chassis design) and Mezger (engine design).

Another to be involved was Norbert Singer, the competitions engineer who master-minded the racing successes of 1973 and 1974, paving the way for the racing versions (934 and 935) which came along for the 1976 season. It usually happens at Porsche that engineers can be working on racing car developments one month and on production car developments the next, a very desirable state of affairs. The Porsche family has always contended that the problems which arise in motor racing, and which have to be solved quickly and effectively, train young engineers to think laterally where necessary, and to develop their initiative in a way that would never be possible in another sphere. All these men had a hand in the 911 Turbo's history, one way or another; none can take all the credit, but all can take some of it.

In typical Porsche fashion the Turbo would be an evolution rather than a revolution, though to the customer it was a transformed machine. It was closely related to the Carrera RS 3.0, a develop-

Far left *Helmuth Flegl, 'father' of the 911 Turbo project*

Left *Norbert Singer, as racing team manager, developed the racing versions*

ment of the classic Carrera 2.7 intended primarily for competitions in 1974/75. For the 1974 racing season Porsche built a batch of 3-litre Carreras— in all, 109 for road use and 50 to racing specification—incorporating all the modifications and improvements that would be needed to keep the car competitive on the world's circuits against potentially more powerful De Tomaso Panteras, Chevrolet Corvettes, Ferrari Daytonas and the like.

Most obviously, the wheel arches were flared substantially to house the wider wheels, 8 in width front and 9 in width rear, with 60-series tyre equipment for road use. The 50 track cars then had the permissible 2 in extensions built into the wheel arches so as to accommodate racing wheels, 10.5 in wide at the front and 14 in wide at the rear. Visually too, the Carrera RS and RSR were identified by the new-style wrap-round fibreglass bumper bars, larger but lighter than those on the Carrera 2.7 by virtue of not being the recoil type and incorporating brake duct cooling holes.

25

Two from the same stable: the roadgoing Porsche Carrera RS (left) and the racing RSR (right). The racer's wider wheels, flared arches and exposed oil cooler are immediate identifications

Two completely new flat-deck rear wings were devised for the 3-litre cars, of the 'tea tray' type. Both were surrounded by flexible foam rubber to satisfy the German licensing authorities, the chief difference being that the wing on the RS (road version) was shorter than that on the RSR.

As it happens, these modifications, especially to the wheel arches, increased the frontal area by nearly 20 per cent (to 1.911 square metres) and the drag coefficient rose to 0.421. Despite an increase in power to 230 horsepower (RS road car) or 330 horsepower in the RSR racing version, the 3-litres were no quicker on a straight road. It was another story though on race tracks and winding public roads where the wider wheels, improved brakes and suspension changes made the 1974 versions altogether much quicker.

Braking was greatly improved with the adoption of 917 type brake discs and four-piston calipers. The discs were fully ventilated and cross-drilled, while the calipers virtually doubled the pad area. In the suspension area, the rear semi-trailing arms had revised fulcrum points to increase the camber change and larger wheel bearings were adopted. Harder settings for the Bilstein shock absorbers and softer adjustable front torsion bars were part of the new specification.

Possibly the most significant development of all for the 3-litre Carrera was the change from sandcast magnesium to die-cast aluminium alloy for the engine crankcase. Magnesium had been the standard base material since 1968, but as the capacities increased by 40 per cent from 2-litres to 2.8-litres by increasing the bores, the crankcase was stretched to its limit and was developing cracks in racing conditions. Aluminium might be heavier but it is more rigid and was better able to resist local stresses, so the 3-litre Carrera had virtually a new power unit. The bore was standardised at 95 mm and the stroke at 70.4 mm, giving a capacity of 2994 cc. New cylinder heads with the stud holes further apart were specified, the camshafts ran in four bearings, and valves were enlarged to 49 mm diameter on the inlet side and 41.5 mm on the exhaust side.

At this point it was decided to raise the compression so as to run on Premium grade fuel. The RS, with 9.8:1 compression, developed 230 bhp DIN at 6200 rpm with 203 lb. ft of torque at 5000 rpm, still using the same valve timing and lift as the previous Carrera. The RSR, on the other hand, had twin-plug heads, 10.5:1 compression and among other competition modifications it adopted throttle slides to control the Bosch mechanical injection system. The output was now

*An original publicity
photograph of the 911 Turbo
showing all the luxury
equipment—recoil bumbers,
electric door mirror, rear
wiper, 15-inch forged alloy
wheels, headlamp washers
and front foglights*

The Group 4 Porsche 934 was ready in time to scoop all the major honours in racing in 1976. For the first time it employed water in the cooling system—in fact to cool the inducted air—and the radiator is in the nose

330 bhp DIN at 8000 rpm, compared with 308 bhp for the previous 2.8-litre racing unit.

Even the 'standard' Carrera RS now had a number of racing components such as uprated crankshaft and connecting rods, a lighter flywheel, the racing brake system with twin

The 'baby' Porsche raced only twice in the 2-litre class, both times in the German National Championship. At the Hockenheim Ring in August 1977 Jacky Ickx led from pole position and almost lapped the field in the race *supporting the German Grand Prix. The 1.4 litre turbocharged engine produced 370 horsepower*

31

master cylinders, a large engine oil cooler mounted at the front, and a limited slip differential (80 per cent locking factor). It would therefore be comparatively easy and inexpensive to convert a road car to full racing trim, and subsequently many of the 109 production versions were partly or fully modified for competitions.

It is surprising to realise that all the 3-litre Carreras were sold by Porsche—they were never actually raced by the factory, yet they were at the time the most successful model ever produced by the company for competitions. In two successive years, 1974 and 1975, privately entered Carreras trounced the opposition in the European Grand Touring Championship and in the American IMSA series, and almost invariably won the Group 4 class in the World Championship endurance races. Among these successes must be recorded a repeat win in the 1975 Daytona 24-hour race by Peter Gregg/Hurley Haywood, recalling their success in 1973 with the previous Carrera.

During 1974 the factory was concerned with developing and race-proving the 2.1-litre prototype Carrera Turbo, as previously described and before the season was out the competitions engineer, Norbert Singer, was satisfied that enough had been learned to apply all the accumulated experience to three new projects known internally as the 930, 934 and 935.

Chapter 3
The first road car

The announcement of the 911 Turbo at the Paris Salon in 1974 was a minor sensation. BMW had previously dabbled with the 2002 Turbo, a 2-litre model, but had decided not to proceed with the project, being more interested in developing the straight-six engine for the racing coupés. But the Porsche was another matter, with its 3-litre engine producing a lusty 260 horsepower and a claim of 155 mph in maximum speed. It would acclerate from standstill to 100 mph in around 14 seconds, an elapsed time which would allow a normal family saloon to reach 60 mph perhaps. The wicked looking flared wheel arches amply covered the 15 in diameter forged-alloy wheels, 7 in width at the front and 8 in width at the rear, and the tea-tray rear spoiler was a direct heritage from the Carrera 3-litre.

As shown in Paris, the Turbo had cross-drilled discs, as used on the Carreras and all the publicity photographs also revealed this type of braking, but in reality the factory was having some problems with hairline cracking and would not put them into production until late in 1977 (1978 model year) when the 3.3-litre engine was introduced.

In other ways too the Turbo was not quite ready for sale. In Paris, for instance, the turbocharger tract was a wooden mock-up, so the car definitely wasn't a runner and even when the car appeared at the Geneva Salon next March the

As shown in pre-production form in 1974 the Turbo had recoil-less bumpers, and an oil cooler was positioned in the nose

stronger four-speed type 930 transmission still wasn't quite ready. Journalists were invited to drive the prototypes on the roads around Geneva, but were asked not to attempt any fierce standing starts! Production did begin in April 1975, and by the time the 1975 model year had run out in

August a total of 273 cars had been produced for the European markets, well on the way to the planned 400 needed for homologation. The price in Britain was a high £14,740, but it included an electric sliding roof—a total of 17 had been ordered by British customers in advance of production, at a time when the luxury car market was suffering from a serious recession in the wake of the first oil crisis.

Not only Britain, but the whole world was suffering to some extent from the shock of the Middle East war and its effect on oil production and price. The Americans were cushioned a little from the crisis, but the other industrialised nations were seriously concerned about energy,

Air ducting for the prototype was somewhat rudimentary, and in Paris this equipment was in fact a mock-up

The notional idea that the Turbo was purely a homologation special for racing development was reinforced by publicity pictures showing the prototype on racing tyres

and it was a distinct act of faith in 1974 for Dr. Fuhrmann to give the go-ahead for a very high performance car, probably fuel-thirsty and decked with luxury items. There was certainly a school of thought at the factory that perhaps Porsche should make 400 for its racing customers and be done with it. To go through with the full production idea, and to aim the Turbo at wealthy and discerning customers who like their comfort was perhaps one of the best decisions Dr. Fuhrmann made in his tenure. He argued: 'As long as cars are made, there will always be people who want something better, something faster. Possibly the last car ever made will be a sports car'. It was this unshakable logic which enabled him to proceed with the 928, which was also undergoing an identity crisis at a critical stage in its development in 1974.

One score on which the Turbo could be criticised was its wheel arches, which increased the total overall width of the car by 4.88 in (to 69.9 in) compared with the Carrera 3. They did appear to be unnecessarily wide for the wheel and tyre equipment supplied (tyres were Pirelli CN36 with 185 section at the front and 215 section at the rear) and indeed they were, but the flares were needed for homologation purposes so that much wider racing wheels could be fitted later on. Spacers were used to bring the wheels out to fill the arches, but Dr. Fuhrmann had the last word by having the Turbo's engine and running gear fitted into a narrower, standard Carrera bodyshell for his personal use ... and this car was a full 10 km/h (6 mph) faster in a straight line!

The power unit itself was a direct descendant of the Carrera 3-litre engine which had acquitted itself so well on the race circuits. The same aluminium block, the same Nikasil cylinders with 95×70.4 mm dimensions were used, giving the

The first 911 Turbo made with right-hand drive was a Porsche Cars Great Britain demonstrator, given a memorable registration number (opposite)

same swept volume of 2994 cc (and this same type 930 engine base would be used on the 1976 model Carrera 3 road car, too). However forged pistons with virtually flat tops were specified in order to lower the compression to 6.5:1, absolutely vital with turbocharging as the effective compression would rise close to 11.5:1 on full boost.

Mechanical injection of the Carreras and the 1974 Le Mans Turbo gave way to Bosch's new K-Jetronic system, in conjunction with the same supplier's electronic ignition system. The K-Jetronic was a real advance, measuring the fuel more precisely against the airflow than the old plunger-pump fuel-injection system and therefore being much 'cleaner' in exhaust emissions, as well as more economical. On the ignition side, the Bosch system completely eliminated the contact breaker which could break, wear out and would need adjustment, replacing this by the new electronic system operated via a trigger disc inside the distributor.

So far as the turbocharging system itself was concerned, all the racing experience on the 911 Carrera could be transferred to the production engine. The turbocharger was a KKK unit (Kühnle, Kopp & Kausch) tucked away behind

Below For the American market, the Turbo was given the appelation 'Turbo Carrera' as it replaced the 911 Carrera model for the States
Below right A fancy line in stick-on lettering has been offered

the left side of the number plate valance, and the system incorporated both the waste-gate to control boost pressure at a maximum of 0.8 bar at 3000 rpm, and a by-pass control which reduced back pressure on the charger when the throttles were closed, thus helping to keep the turbo blade speed up and reduce throttle lag.

The early cars had a tendency for their American Garrett wastegates to jam if they had been parked for a few days, leading to a sudden increase in boost pressure and dramatic surges in

In production form the Turbo was considerably more refined, especially at the rear, with heavy rubber overriders on the recoil bumpers offering good protection against parking knocks. The British market versions had every possible 'extra' in the price

The Turbo's 3-litre engine was slightly detuned (245 horsepower against 260 for Europe) for the American market, thanks to the detox emission equipment—but it was still a mighty impressive car

power. Fortunately the designers were wise to this and fitted an overboost safety switch adjustment to 1.1 to 1.4 bar, cutting off the fuel pumps and saving the owner from having an expensive repair bill (either to his engine or the bodywork, depending on circumstances).

On the transmission side, an entirely new gearbox (type 930) was designed of just four gears instead of five; their wider teeth could now cope with the massive power and torque. As an example, the older five-speed type 915 box was on its limit—beyond it, really—at 450 horsepower in the much lightened racing car, and would have been equally stretched on the near 1200 kg road car albeit with less power. The 930 transmission on the other hand was easily able to cope with 750 horsepower, which was ultimately attained from the 935/78 racing car, and failures in road cars are almost unheard of.

The clutch diameter was increased from 225 to 240 mm, and this also necessitated the adoption of a larger flywheel. On the suspension side the rear 'banana' trailing arms, made of cast alloy, allowed the use of larger tapered roller wheel bearings; Bilstein shock absorbers were fitted, certainly endowing the Turbo with a harder than usual ride but giving the degree of control that an owner would require, and some anti-dive was built into the suspension geometry for smoother, flatter braking.

The development programme had gone quite smoothly, considering the complexity of the task in hand. The first prototype of the Turbo to run in 1974 was a Carrera R10 (research vehicle number 10) with a turbocharged engine but with normal

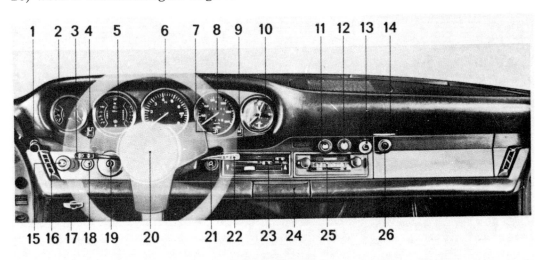

1 Release for fuel tank filler flap	10 Clock	19 Ignition/starter switch and steering lock
2 Fuel/oil level gauge	11 Rear window defogger switch	20 Horn
3 Turn signal/headlight dimmer switch	12 Fog light switch	21 Interval operation switch
4 Rear windshield wiper switch	13 Cigarette lighter	22 Wiper/washer lever
5 Oil temperature/pressure gauge	14 Glove compartment light	23 Heating and ventilation controls
6 Tachometer	15 Light switch	24 Ashtray
7 Trip odometer reset control	16 Defroster jet	25 Radio
8 Speedometer	17 Front hood release	26 Glove compartment lock
9 Headlight washer switch	18 Emergency flasher switch	

Carrera rear suspension. It was the wider wheels which caused most problems, firstly with the wheel bearings which had to be replaced by wider and larger roller-type Timken bearings, and secondly with the lack of body strength, a problem which had to be cured by an extra welding process. In fact two Targa versions were built during the programme, but these were thought not to be stiff enough (by Porsche's rigorous standards) so the factory never proceeded with this, though the German b+b specialist company did offer Targa versions with specially strengthened bodies.

Braking, as mentioned, also caused headaches as the cross-drilled discs were prone to cracking

The addition of the air conditioning pump on the right side of the engine just about filled the last available space in the engine compartment, hiding one bank of cylinders

when put through a rigorous test schedule involving 200 consecutive applications from maximum speed down to 100 km/h (62 mph)! This sort of usage might never be needed by a customer, but it is typical of Porsche's thoroughness to keep the design out of production until it had been sorted out.

As anticipated, the type 915 5-speed gearbox was nowhere near strong enough for the job. It was found that the prototype R10 oversteered rather strongly and this was cured by changing the rear pickup points for the semi-trailing arms and playing around with the torsion bar and roll-bar rates; at the same time the front anti-dive characteristic under braking was increased.

The centre console carried controls for the air-conditioning, storage for cassette tapes, and at the whim of the owner a radio-telephone as well

So, with a power output of 260 horsepower DIN at 5500 rpm, coupled with 286 lb. ft of torque at 4000 rpm, Porsche had produced one of the world's most desirable road cars—lavishly equipped, undeniably expensive, but very, very fast... and safe.

In the 1976 model year (September 1975 to August 1976) a total of 1201 Turbos were built: 519 for the United States, where they were sold as '911 Carrera Turbo' and were rated at 245 horsepower with full exhaust emission equipment, 653 for the 'rest of the world' (including 28 for Japan), and 29 Group 4 934 Turbo RSR racing models. Production peaked in the 1977 model year at 1722 examples built, including 716 for America, 985 for the rest of the world (including 49 to Japanese specification), nine more Group 4 cars and a dozen type 935 Group 5 cars for customers.

For 1978 there was a second, and probably final major development when the engine capacity was raised to 3299 cc by means of boring and stroking the power unit to 97 × 74.4 mm. Larger diameter main and big-end bearings were fitted and the compression ratio increased to 7.0:1. The most important modification of all, though, was the installation of an air-to-air intercooler which lowered the temperature of the compressed air by 50 to 60 degrees Centrigrade before it entered the manifold, thus improving the engine's volumetric efficiency. Accompanying the intercooler was a new, bigger and aerodynamically more efficient rear wing, this time with a grille incorporated to duct air onto the intercooler.

Now the power output of the 'world' version rose to 300 horsepower, and torque to 304 lb. ft over a wider range of engine speeds, improving the acceleration and lifting the car's maximum

In the early stages of development more blades were added to the fan to increase capacity and to reduce the noise level. The big plastic box on top of the engine is nothing more than an induction/filter housing

speed to 161 mph. Along with the engine modification, the clutch plate was redesigned, cushion-
ing the power take-up but at the same time
reducing the gearbox 'chatter' at low speeds. This
hub, being thicker than the original disc, entailed
moving the engine back three centimetres in the
body, and there was a weight penalty of around
30 kg (66 lb) too on account of the clutch and
intercooler. To cope with this and the higher top
speed, the recommended tyre pressures at the rear
went up from 2.4 to 3 bar (33 to 42 lb), so that the
change in handling characteristics would be
almost imperceptible to the average owner.
Among those to have contributed to the development was a British engineer, John Wheeler, in
charge of chassis development on the 911 and
Turbo from 1977 to 1980.

In common with the 911 SC model, the Turbo
was now equipped with a brake servo which
intruded a little into the front luggage compartment. It proved no hardship for the keener drivers

*A closer view of the impact
bumpers, which have recoil
dampers hidden behind the
'banjo' rubber in order to
minimise damage. Note
single exhaust for the 3-litre*

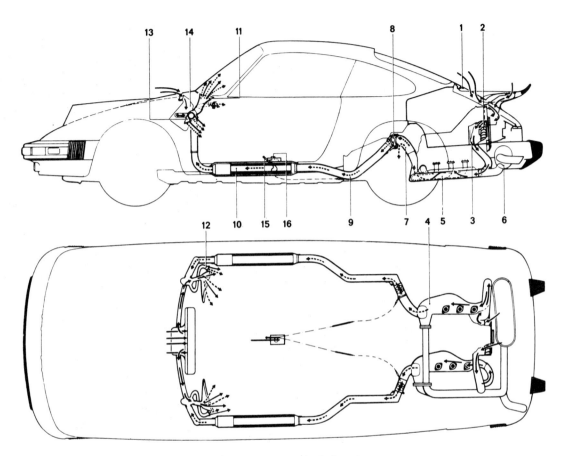

but a boon for lady drivers and those who drive in town for a proportion of their time, overcoming the very wooden feel of the brake pedal at low speeds and when the discs were cold. At this time the Turbo was fitted, in production, with new Porsche designed Alcan calipers and the long-awaited type 917 cross-drilled discs. At last the road car really did have racing car brake performance.

Production dropped back in the 1978 model year to 1248 cars, partly because the revised Turbo didn't start going down the line until October, comprising 450 for America, 50 for

From the driver's manual—a diagramatic view of the sophisticated heating and ventilation system showing how air is passed through the heat exchangers and taken into the cabin. A centrally placed electro switch on the tunnel is used to dial the required air temperature, automatic sensors keeping the level constant

Japan, 724 for the rest of the world, and 24 more 935 racing cars for customers.

Figures for the 1979 model year are distorted because the model was discontinued for the States in December 1979 on account of still stricter emission requirements. Therefore the run of 1979 model chassis numbers was extended through the autumn for the American market only, 805 being built for the US up to August and a further 384 in the autumn. Putting together the 1979 and 1980 model years a total of 2891 cars were built in Zuffenhausen.

The final modification to be mentioned is a new and more efficient exhaust system with twin tailpipes, introduced for the 911 Turbo in September 1979. An improved oil cooler was fitted to the Turbo and the 911 SC, but the performance characteristics remained unchanged.

In describing the evolution of the Turbo, it should be mentioned that after a few months the original Pirelli CN36 tyres were superseded by the lower, wider Pirelli P7 equipment which had been developed by Pirelli and Porsche engineers in the splendid Weissach test facility. With a 50 per cent aspect ratio (the sidewall height being half the tread width) the P7 was originally fitted onto the same 15 in diameter rim, later onto a similar but bigger one-inch rim, 16 in in diameter. The tyre widths were increased to 205 section at the front and 225 section at the rear.

The car's handling was greatly improved and so much more grip was available that the rear wheels could not now be made to break adhesion on a dry tarmac surface, so it was the clutch that burned in a fierce start. Road test figures suffered therefore, until the improved clutch mechanism of the 3.3-litre model, coupled with higher tyre pressures and better engine characteristics, once again made it possible to spin the wheels.

Chapter 4
The racers

Little space is allocated in this book for the racing cars, but the Turbo story would not be complete without a brief description of the car which dominated World Championship racing from 1976 to 1981, and actually won the classic 24 Hours of Le Mans in 1979.

Norbert Singer, the engineer/team manager who took the 911 Carrera Turbo racing car through its vital development period on the circuit in 1974, was responsible for all 935 development while Wolfgang Berger (later senior head of quality control at Zuffenhausen) was in charge of the 934 project. In case there is any confusion, the 934 was intended for Group 4 (GT) racing and the 935 for Group 5 World Championship events. The 936, an open prototype car still using the same basic 911 flat-6 engine, was designed for Group 6 events.

Taking the 934 customer car first, it closely resembled the 911 Turbo road car, right down to the electric windows and most of the luxury trim, for under the new regulations the weight of the car was dictated by the engine capacity. With the 1.4 multiplication applied, the 3-litre turbo engine was rated by the CSI at 4.2-litres, so the car had to weigh at least 1120 kg—and to achieve this it raced with 40 kg of lead ballast installed!

The power unit was uprated to a healthy 485 horsepower quite easily. The compression ratio remained at 6.5:1 and Bosch K-Jetronic injection was retained as was the contactless ignition. However the boost pressure was raised to 1.4 bar and volumetric efficiency was greatly improved by fitting a water-cooled intercooler, the water radiator being fitted in the nose of the car. Wide, 16 in diameter wheels were fitted for racing and a total of 38 such vehicles were built at an asking price of 97,000 Deutschemarks. Immediately the 934 took over from the Carrera RSR as the pace-setter, an almost certain Group 4 class winner wherever it appeared. Toine Hezemans won the European GT Championship in a 934 in 1976 and George Follmer the American Trans-Am series— and in 1979 a 934 finished as high as fourth at Le Mans, behind a trio of 935s.

The 935 was quite a different animal. It was still based on the 911 Turbo, as indeed it had to be, but the standard bodywork was extensively clad in figure-hugging fibreglass which smoothed the lines and made it faster in a straight line. Two

During 1974 the cooling fan was moved to the horizontal for racing, to improve the cooling of the rearmost cylinders

different nose forms were used in 1976, the 'faster' of the two actually relocating the headlights lower down.

Torsion bar suspension was replaced by titanium coil springs, an alloy frame stiffened the front compartment, and of course the car was substantially lightened. The engine capacity was taken back to 2856 cc (by reducing the bore to 92.8 mm) so as to fall in the under 4-litre class for racing after the 1.4 multiplication factor had been applied, and the minimum weight of the car would have to be 970 kg. In fact the first 935 raced with 90 kg of lead ballast distributed at the front and

With BBS racing wheels fitted the 934 racing car looked aggressive without losing its attractive lines. A deep air dam helped to improve stability, but the standard rear spoiler had to be retained

On show in Geneva in 1977, the customer versions of the 935 (Group 5) silhouette racing car showed just how the bodywork could be improved aerodynamically without infringing the rules. In particular, the rear wings were substantially widened around the normal bodyshell

on the floor in order to adjust the centre of gravity, so easy was it for Porsche to meet the rules.

Wheel width regulations were rather restrictive for a car developing nearly 600 horsepower and Porsche got around this problem in an intriguing way : instead of putting more rubber on the road with wider tyres, a route which was blocked by the rules, they enlarged the tyre contact area (footprint) simply by fitting extra tall rear wheels of 19 in diameter, in collaboration with Dunlop who provided some ultra low-profile tyres for the job.

Engine power was raised substantially, even compared with the 934, by means of fitting twin-plug heads of similar design to the earlier Carrera's, an air-to-air intercooler (which had to

By 1978 the 935 was converted to twin turbocharger application, in order to improve the pickup and further reduce throttle lag. Power rose slightly and the car was easier to drive. Denuded of its extra bodywork, the 935 is not so different from its production counterpart

Porsche's ultimate 935 was the /78 model, raced only twice. With water cooled, four-valve cylinder heads the power was 750 horsepower, and the car won its debut race at Silverstone. At Le Mans it was delayed, finishing seventh. 'Moby Dick' pushed the regulations to their limit!

be changed at short notice midway through the first season, because it possibly infringed the rules, to a water-cooled type), reverting to mechanical injection, and by increasing the maximum permitted engine speed to 7900 rpm. It was officially quoted by Porsche as producing 590 bhp, rising to 630 bhp for the 1977 racing season when twin turbochargers were fitted.

In 1978 there was a further, quite startling development called (appropriately enough) the 935/78. This car, developed by Singer and his team stretched the rules to the limit, and was soon dubbed 'Moby Dick' on account of its whale-like appearance. Any resemblance to a 911 was almost incidental, for the front and rear sections were chopped off to be replaced by space-frame struc-

57

The ultimate success for the Porsche 935 was to win Le Mans in 1979, the Kremer prepared car driven by Klaus Ludwig, Don and Bill Whittington

The 936 programme was a late decision reached during the previous winter to counter Renault's bid for the World Sportscar Championship, but it paid handsome dividends with outright wins at Le Mans in 1976, 1977 and again in 1981. The car still used Porsche's ubiquitous 6-cylinder production engine in 2.2 litre form

tures and the floor was cut out and replaced by another frame at door sill level thus lowering the entire body by some three inches!

The engine, too, was startlingly different in having water-cooled cylinder heads in the quest for higher efficiency and greater power. It had long been realised that, with air cooling, large valves were *de rigueur* but they were necessarily heavy and limited engine speed. As far back as 1970, experiments had been carried out with water-cooled cylinder head and now the exercise reached reality ... simply, with water cooling (but still air cooling for the cylinders) four smaller valves would fit into the heads without problems, these being more efficient and permitting the engine speed to rise to 8200 rpm. Now the power shot up to a conservatively quoted 750

horsepower and the 935/78 proved an astonishingly rapid car even against other 935s. It won the Silverstone 6-hours with ease on its debut, but suffered minor problems—including a misfire that went on all night—at Le Mans, finishing well down in eighth place. However, it was some nine seconds per lap faster than the previous year's works car and more than 20 mph faster on the Mulsanne Straight, peaking at 227 mph during practice, so the point was well made to potential rivals. Possibly BMW had been thinking of challenging Porsche again in the World Championship, but that show of strength put any such thoughts out of the Munich company's head.

Suffice it to say that the 935 won the World Championship for Manufacturers in 1976, in 1977, in 1978 and again in 1979, this last year also seeing

No production car base has been taken further than the 'final' 935/78. Interpretation of the rule book has never been more skilfull

the production-based 935 scoring an outright win at Le Mans. By 1980 however the factory had ceased all development on rear-engined cars in order to concentrate on the 924 Carrera GT, and even such a good customer as Erwin Kremer was not quite able to hold off a determined bid for the World Championship by Lancia.

One remarkable development which took the motor racing world by surprise was the 'Baby Turbo' which ran twice during the 1977 season in the 2-litre class. Porsche had raced many times in the 2-litre division, but the mandatory equivalency factor on a turbocharged engine dictated that the swept capacity should not exceed 1425 cc. In record time the engineers developed the smallest flat-6 ever which, with turbocharging, developed no less than 370 horsepower. This power unit was installed in a much lightened 935 bodyshell, reduced to 750 kg (the minimum for the class was 735 kg) and Jacky Ickx gave the car its debut at the Norisring in a German championship event. Such was the ambient temperature and the lack of insulation from the engine, that Ickx had to retire, but at the Hockenheim Ring a few weeks later the brilliant Belgian driver recorded a flag-to-flag victory, almost lapping the entire field.

Mention should be made too of the 936 prototype racing car, which used a version of the 1974 2142 cc turbo engine to win at Le Mans in 1976 and again in 1977. A similar power unit of 2650 cc capacity and running on methanol was also prepared for Indianapolis in 1980, this producing 630 horsepower at 9000 rpm. Sadly though, Porsche became emrboiled in the heated politics surrounding Indy and the engine, installed in an Interscope team car, never appeared on a starting grid.

Chapter 5
On the road

The lithe, muscular lines of the Porsche Turbo are
enough to pump adrenalin into the blood of a
sports car enthusiast even before the ignition key
is turned . . . it's an aggressive looking machine
packed with power. Open up the engine compartment and it is crowded with machinery, the dry-
sump flat-6 engine virtually hidden by the cooling
fan, the air pump, the air conditioning unit (when
fitted) and (since 1978) the intercooler. If you
wanted to change the plugs you'd first have to find
them, a job better left to Porsche-trained mechanics. But that is not really important, because all
Porsche's six and eight-cylinder engines have
12,000 mile service intervals and are remarkably
untemperamental, so it is better to leave them to
those who know what they are doing!

To some, the description of a sports car would
suggest a cramped, draughty animal that demanded tolerance from its owner, but that is
definitely not true of any Porsche. These German
made cars are renowned for their fine coachwork,
excellent paint finish, quietness of operation and
general sophistication, and none more so than the
Turbo.

Turn the ignition key (it even has a little light
in the handle so that you can insert it neatly in the
dark) and leave the accelerator pedal alone . . .
the motor should fire immediately, the Bosch
K-Jetronic injection system taking care of the
cold start mixture automatically. The engine will

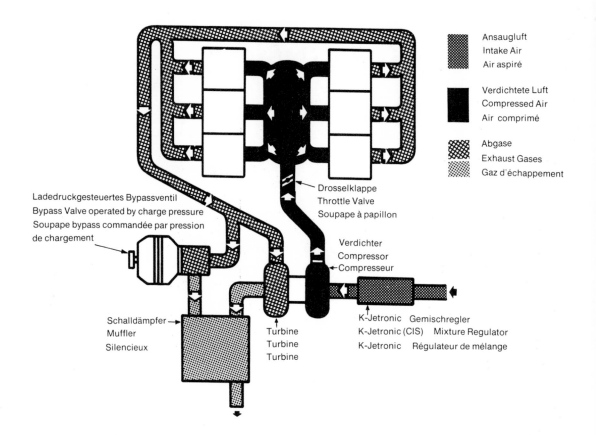

Ansaugluft
Intake Air
Air aspiré

Verdichtete Luft
Compressed Air
Air comprimé

Abgase
Exhaust Gases
Gaz d'échappement

Ladedruckgesteuertes Bypassventil
Bypass Valve operated by charge pressure
Soupape bypass commandée par pression
de chargement

Drosselklappe
Throttle Valve
Soupape à papillon

Verdichter
Compressor
Compresseur

Schalldämpfer
Muffler
Silencieux

Turbine
Turbine
Turbine

K-Jetronic   Gemischregler
K-Jetronic (CIS)   Mixture Regulator
K-Jetronic   Régulateur de mélange

An everyman's guide to turbocharging; an illustration from a 911 Turbo brochure showing just how the system works

settle down to a muted rumble at the back, awaiting further instructions. Unlike some rivals the Turbo's clutch is light and easy to operate—it has a helper spring which gives a distinct 'up and over' feel when the pedal is depressed—and the rather long but handily placed gear lever has a precise feel about it.

The Turbo is indeed an easy car to drive around quietly, making no demands on the Monday morning commuter, or his wife. With stereo and air conditioning switched on it's as suitable as any family saloon for routine work in heavy traffic, and envying glances should make the owner satisfied with his choice. The Turbo

Outwardly similar in appearance to the 911 model which had gone into production previously, the Turbo model now boasted 260 horsepower—twice the original output—and a top speed in excess of 150 mph

Above *Flared wheel arches, an air dam, and a distinctive rear 'wing' all help to provide downforce and adhesion in keeping with the Turbo's supercar performance*

Left *Tail view of two 'turbochargers' (left): a 3-litre Turbo, and 1981 2-litre 924 Carrera GT. They represent a marked contrast in styles, one with a rear engine and air cooling, the 924 with a front engine and water cooling*

Right *Porsche's flagship became a real classic in 3.3 litre form (right) when the power rose to 300 hp*

Above *The 3.3 litre model (above) was quoted by* Motor *magazine as being the fastest production car to pass through their hands, but ultra-high speeds are ably coped with by the racing brake system, Pirelli P7 tyres and efficient aerodynamics*

Right *In contemporary form the 911 Turbo features twin exhaust pipes, slightly improving the efficiency of the exhaust system. This was Porsche Cars' (GB) demonstrator model in 1980, with light blue wheels matching the leather upholstery*

RBH 699W

Above *Various customizers have changed the 911 Turbo*

Right *The original objective in making the Turbo was to run a works Group 5 Porsche in the 1976 World Championship for Manufacturers. Jacky Ickx and Jochen Mass enjoyed a splendid season in the Martini 935*

Left *Sensual lines of the 3-litre Turbo; the wheel arches being exaggerated to allow the homologation of wider wheels for racing*

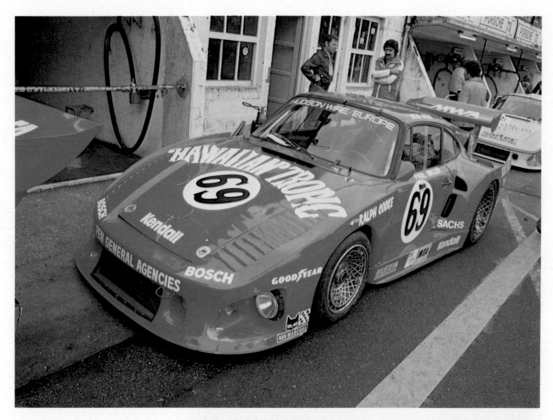

Above *When the factory ceased development on the 935 model in 1978 the work was taken up by Erwin Kremer, whose K3 model won outright at Le Mans in 1979*

Right *For road work, Kremer offers a stunning 'Group 5 Street R' version of the Turbo, embodying many of the visual features of the racing car. The dropaway fenders and reprofiled nose improve the drag coefficient suffiently to raise the maximum speed by some 12 mph*

wouldn't miss a beat on a hot summer's day in London or Paris traffic, though the luxury of leather upholstery can be a mixed blessing in the summertime unless the air conditioning is employed.

Out of town the Turbo shows the reverse side of its Jekyll and Hyde character. Approaching 3000 revs per minute in the original 3-litre car a faint whistle became apparent, with a sudden surge of power pinning the occupants back in their seats. Floor the throttle and, suddenly, your leather-trimmed cockpit becomes the console of a racing car as the rev-counter flashes round to the red line at 6800 rpm and the rev-limiter stutters into action. In first gear the car would now be travelling at 53 mph, and repeating the treatment in second gear would swing the speedometer round to 90 mph; given the space, third gear would propel the car to 127 mph, and only then in top gear would the onward rush be subdued. On a motorway 140 mph could be achieved quickly—very quickly indeed—but the last 15 mph to maximum speed would take a little longer. Denis Jenkinson described the car as having a very high 'Oh-my-Gawd factor', the sort of feeling you get when you tread the throttle pedal for the first time in anger and feel your breath taken away by the sheer response!

Journalists were able to drive the Turbo for the first time from the Geneva Show in March 1975, and PR chief Manfred Jantke entrusted one of his press cars to myself, fellow journalist Jeff Hutchinson, and Grand Prix driver Jack Oliver who lost no time in involving himself in the action. We let Jack do the driving, reckoning that he would know how to master this machine, and soon the Turbo was catapulting up the Lausanne autoroute at some extremely illegal speeds. After winding the speedometer around to 260 km/h

The official power and torque graphs for the 3-litre Turbo, showing its advantages over the 2.7 litre mechanically injected Carrera

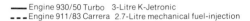

—— Engine 930/50 Turbo   3-Litre K-Jetronic
- - - Engine 911/83 Carrera 2.7-Litre mechanical fuel-injection

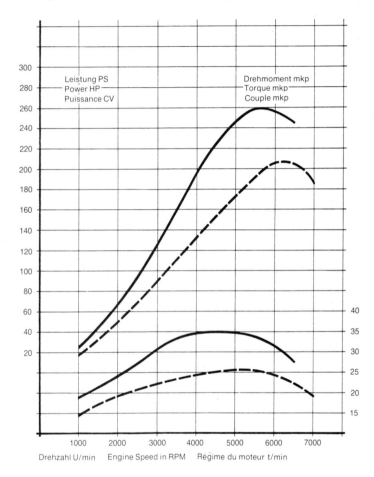

(160 mph) we decided that discretion was the better part of valour and headed for the mountains where some 'point and squirt' motoring on partly icy roads kept us amused for at least half an hour before we remembered to stop for a photo session. Before we returned the car we managed to snap off the gear lever knob, a hollowed out plastic fitment, a mishap which wasn't exactly unheard of in the early days.

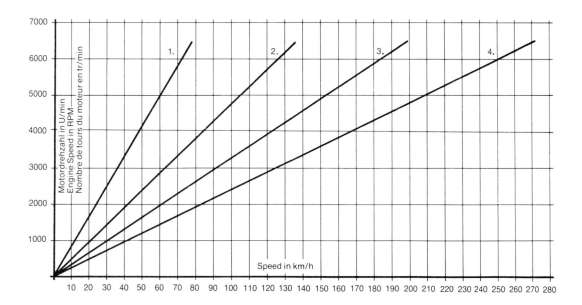

Motordrehzahl in U/min
Engine Speed in RPM
Nombre de tours du moteur en tr/min

Speed in km/h

That hour's session was one of the most exhilarating of my motoring career, matching a 170 mph run round the MIRA test track a few years before, with John Horsman at the wheel of a GT40. There was no question, then, that the Porsche Turbo had been designed for wealthy customers searching for the ultimate in motoring experience.

The car's general handling was faultless within its limits, but always demanded respect. Years of engineering had all but eliminated the inherent disadvantage of placing the engine in the tail, and 60 per cent of the weight over the rear wheels. The front air dam and rear wing reduced the 'lift factor' at maximum speed from close on 400 lb to a mere 37 lb, pinning the car firmly to the ground. Not only did this make the Turbo far more stable than a 911 at speeds in excess of 100 mph, but it was also less prone to aquaplaning on standing water and less sensitive to sidewinds.

Development had made the car a natural

Gear charts for the Turbo show the wide spacing dictated by the four-speed layout. With a true maximum of 250 km/h (155 mph) there is plenty in hand in top gear

Above *In terms of
appearance alone the 1974
2.7-litre Carrera was as far
as the factory could go
without excessive
aerodynamic aids*
Right *The next stage was the
more 'cluttered', but more
modern 911 Turbo in 3-litre
form.*

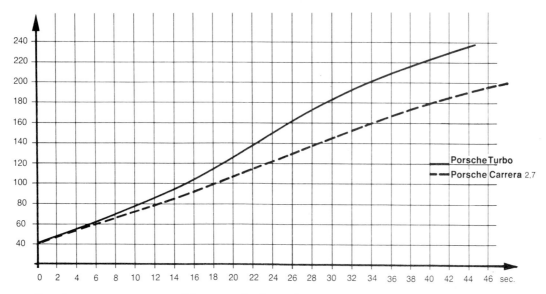

The difference in acceleration between a 3-litre Turbo and a 2.7 litre Carrera is marginal up to 60 mph, but the gap widens rapidly as the extra power and torque of the turbo motor tells. On the road, the difference was amazing

understeerer at reasonable speeds, but the maxim of 'slow in and fast out' was never more true. Driven intelligently the Turbo would reward its owner, but it refused to help if driven into a corner too quickly. A moment's hesitation from the driver would have the tail snapping round, either to spin the car or to put it into a lurid pendulous motion which could end up in the scenery. It always reminded me of a big, lively hunter which had the heart and stamina to chase a fox to the ends of the earth, but would soon ditch an inexperienced rider. The rather sudden entry of the turbocharger at 3000 rpm was no help, either, on the early customer cars. Pressing on, even with caution, was all very well but if one was negotiating a slippery roundabout in second gear the rev-counter would need attention because all hell could break loose when the boosted power was released.

I may have made the car sound like a real beast, but treated with the correct respect the Turbo was, and certainly is now, perfectly safe in

Front and rear suspension of the 3-litre Turbo, from the driver's manual. Aluminium castings were largely used for the steering rack, suspension arms, and of course the engine and gearbox, the suspension medium being torsion bars

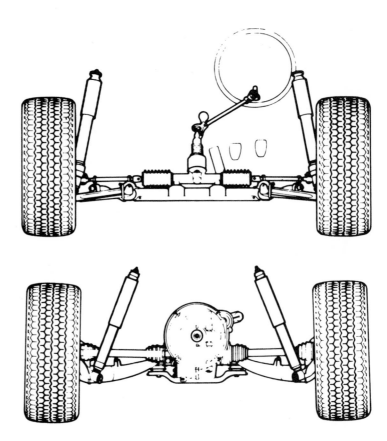

the right hands. Owners had to realise that they had racing car power under their right feet, and should no more press their luck on the public highway than they would in a similarly powered Formula 2 car. People who can afford a Turbo are, normally, responsible individuals (and it has to be said that many of them would buy a Turbo as a success symbol, never caring to seek its limits), and accidents were in fact rarely heard of.

To match this immense performance the brakes had to be superb. Until 1977 the Turbo, in common with other 911s, had no servo unit for its massive 12 in ventilated discs, so they felt rather heavy and unresponsive when cold, especially at

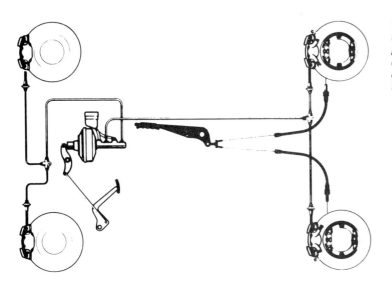

The Turbo's brake circuit. In usual Porsche tradition, good handbrake efficiency is achieved by installing small drums within the rear disc brakes

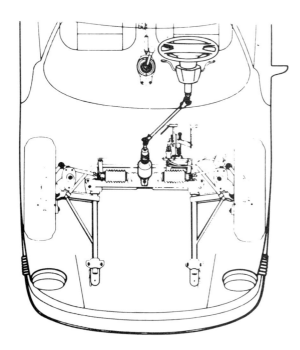

The longitudinal torsion bars illustrating how much valuable luggage space could be saved. The steering rack has a central pickup facilitating right-hand drive production

low speeds—if customers had anything to complain about it was this. Once up to their working temperature, though, it was a different story, these discs providing the cliché-d 'giant hand' retardation; easy 1 g retardation would press the occupants hard against their seat belts and kill the speed smoothly and safely, time and again. To say that they were absolutely fade-free might be a slight exaggeration, for those who hammered their Turbos hard in traffic-free conditions (especially the German customers, it might be said) still wished that they had the cross-drilled discs originally promised.

With only 40 per cent of the weight at the front the steering was reasonably light, except at parking speed, and extremely precise. Rack and pinion steering is generally accepted as being the best and the only shortfall was apparent at very low speed when the 185 section Pirelli Cinturatos fitted at the front offered real resistance to turning moment. Springing, remember, was still by means of torsion bars just as Professor Porsche's VW Beetle had been designed 40 years before.

For the 1976 model year (commencing August 1975) Pirelli P7 tyre equipment became available at a quoted extra price of DM 800, though a standard fitting for the British market. These radial-ply tyres, hand-finished and considerably more expensive than mass production tyres, had been developed by Pirelli and Porsche engineers at Weissach on Porche's unique 4.5-metre drum, on which the tyres can be run inside the perimeter rather than on top of a rolling road surface. Its construction resembling that of a racing tyre, the P7 was the last word in road tyre equipment and truly matched the capabilities of the Porsche Turbo. The wheel diameter remained at 15 in and a new speedometer had to be fitted to compensate

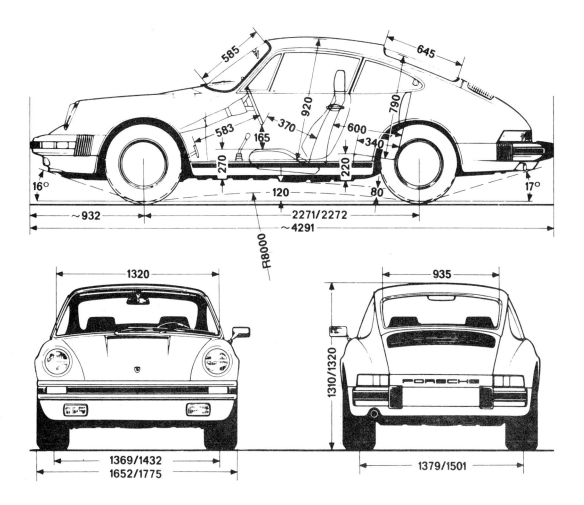

for the 50 per cent tyre profile; the tyre sections increased to 205 at the front end and 225 at the rear.

Proving that the Turbo was an entirely practical car, Porsche now offered a year's warranty on mechanical parts irrespective of mileage, and a six-year warranty on the body frame which was made of Thyssen galvanised steel.

Early in the 1976 model year (November 1975

All the vital statistics of the 911 family (taken from a Turbo brochure). The 911 Turbo is rare among the exotica in offering space in the back for children—or extra luggage

81

for America and March 1976 for Europe, to be exact) an air pump was installed to inject fresh air in volume into the exhaust manifolds in order to clean up (or at least dilute) the exhaust emissions. It was more than coincidental that the air pump helped to keep the turbocharger speed up and made it more progressive, so that the boosted inlet charge started 500 rpm sooner (2500 rpm) and less suddenly. This, in itself, made the Turbo distinctly more pleasant to drive.

In the 1977 model year, left-hand drive customers were given the luxury of a brake servo, but British customers had to wait another year while the right-hand drive installation was worked out. There were compensations, though. The heating and ventilation system, for example, was much better in the latest Turbo: automatic temperature control and twin swivelling air vents installed in the centre of the fascia answering a long-standing criticism; the fresh air blower controls were separated, and the cold/warm air control illuminated. Wheel rim diameters went up to 16 in, increasing the tyre contact area, and Pirelli P7 tyres became standard equipment.

Other improvements included thief-proof door locks with turn knobs set into the door lining (in Italy, particularly, no Turbo was safe for five minutes at the kerbside), a centre console, a two-stage electrically heated rear window, a driver's side exterior mirror with electric heating and control mechanism (optional for the passenger side as well), a rear window wiper, and, intriguingly, a boost gauge inset into the rev-counter. The engine's fuel system was improved, as was the gearbox synchromesh; a single 20 mm front anti-roll bar replaced the original three-piece bar, and various detail improvements were carried out to the suspension.

A special version of the 911 Turbo was

prepared for the Motor Show at Earls Court in October, finished in Grand Prix White with Martini stripes along its flanks to commemorate the successful liaison between Porsche and Martini on the world's race circuits. Inevitably this was quickly dubbed 'the Martini Turbo' though it was never officially described as such and eager customers ordered replicas. So popular was the visual appeal that a number of similar 911 and 911 Sport models were built, though the 'Dr. Fuhrmann seats' at £800 a pair were not in such demand. With red, white and blue leather block panels the seats really were the last word in comfort, though it has to be admitted that the

The car which won the World Championship for Makes in 1976 and again in 1977, the type 935 which the Porsche factory raced with support from Martini & Rossi (note the often copied striping). The car is now dubbed the 'taxi' and is used to give important visitors a thrill on the test track at Weissach (and it is marvellously untemperamental!)

83

A rather special Turbo was the so-called 'Martini Turbo' imported for the 1976 Earls Court Motor Show. With the drinks company's stripes on Grand Prix White bodywork it looked stunning, and a number of replicas were sold

whole package was rather startling and took some getting used to!

The show car, which became the press demonstrator, was an instant classic and never failed to impress (it was even used as a wedding car by *Autocar*'s sports editor, Peter Windsor). With its smoother transition to full power—and the boost gauge to tell the driver that extra help was on the way—its P7 tyres, its improved ventilation and obvious refinement the 77 Turbo 3-litre was never less than a joy to drive. Throttle lag was virtually indescernible in normal usage, and the Turbo simply offered extra power if the driver wanted it. One slight debit, maybe, was the less effective engine retardation due to the turbo installation, but this was not serious enough to be called a problem and the customer very quickly came to terms with it.

The early cars on Pirelli Cinturatos had spun their wheels easily enough in fierce starts, but the advent of P7s had glued the Turbo's rear wheels to smooth, dry tarmac and now the clutches would take a pounding in the hands of an over-enthusiastic driver. Road test figures pointed this out, the Turbo being fractionally slower to 60 mph (6.1 seconds in the hands of *Autocar*) than the old 2.7 litre 911 Carrera (5.7 seconds by the same publication).

No owner who cared for his car would ever dream of starting his car from rest in the manner employed by magazines striving for ultimate figures . . . thank goodness. The smell of burning clutch isn't exactly pleasant, lingering in the car for days afterwards, and it comes a bit expensive too. Part of the problem was that if the engine speed dropped, and the turbo wasn't operating, not very much power was being developed and performance suffered accordingly.

Much better therefore—and hardly any slower—to start the car off normally in first gear and not be impatient in that odd half-second it took for the revs to build up. That way 60 mph could regularly be achieved in 6.5 seconds or thereabouts without causing any damage to the clutch. Of course, the appeal of the Turbo has nothing to do with its capabilities off the start-line: the real beauty of the car is the way that it will accelerate from 60 to 100 mph in little more than seven seconds, devouring a line of traffic as if it didn't exist.

Chapter 6
3.3 litres

The last major development to the 911 Turbo was the introduction of the 3.3-litre engine, which transformed the whole car from outstanding to ultimate in road performance.

It was announced in August 1977 that the 1978 model would have 300 horsepower available (265 for America) raising the maximum speed to slightly over 160 miles per hour. A good deal of work was carried out to achieve this, for the bore and stroke dimensions were increased to 97×74.4 mm giving a swept volume of 3299 cc. A new crankshaft and larger main and connecting rod bearings were installed to take the extra power, and the opportunity was taken to increase the compression ratio from 6.5 to 7.0:1. This was possible because an air-to-air intercooler was now fitted, lowering the temperature of the induction air by 50 to 60 degrees Centigrade and increasing the engine's volumetric efficiency.

The intercooler, long since recognised as vital for racing purposes, was now employed to give the customer 'something for nothing', for the power and torque increased by more than the rise in engine size would have suggested. To illustrate this, the swept volume was increased by 10 per cent, the power by 15.4 per cent and the torque by no less than 20 per cent (from 254 lb. ft at 4000 rpm to 304 lb. ft at the same engine speed).

Unusually in a production engine the cylinder

Full-power Curve

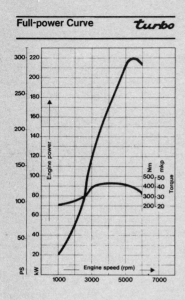

Acceleration Curve

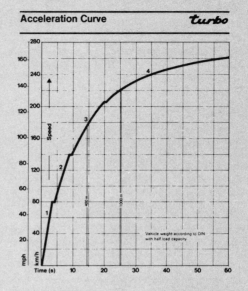

Transmission Diagram
4-speed-transmission type 930/34

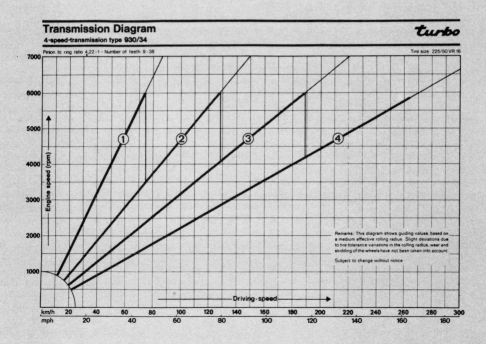

head gaskets were now dispensed with entirely, the heads seating straight onto the finned Nikasil cylinder blocks. The cooling fan speed was increased to 1.8 times crankshaft speed: in the interests of reliability a larger oil pump was fitted and an improved timing chain tensioner finally cured an historically noted problem with the production six-cylinder engine.

The brake system was completely revised, with thicker cross-drilled, internally ventilated discs front and rear fitted with the latest Alcan four-piston calipers and measuring up in every way to the racing car standards expected. The provision of a servo for all markets (new for

Above *How to light up a Christmas tree! Tail lights, brake lights, indicators, reversing lights, twin reflectors, twin rear foglights, not forgetting the number plate bulbs, would dazzle the onlooker if they all came on together*

Opposite *No chrome to be seen. Matt black finish is a Porsche speciality*

The rear wing shape is the only positive identification of the Turbo 3.3 though a closer look at the drilled brake discs and Porsche scripted Alcan calipers is further confirmation

The full-width rear spoiler has a greater grille area to serve the new intercooler, and the air conditioning radiator. Also the later spoiler further increases the rear downforce at speed

Britain, and increased in size compared with the previous year) was by now a necessity, for without it the brakes would have been intolerably heavy. The 'traditionalists' who frowned on the very idea of servo brakes for a Porsche need not have worried, for the servo assistance was immediate and quite subtle, and soon no 911 owner would want to be without this aid.

A new type of Porsche-designed clutch was installed at the same time, featuring an improved but thicker diaphragm spring mechanism which increased the grip on the plates and completely

eliminated the rather characteristic gear 'chatter' which was always noticed at low engine speeds, on a light throttle. The new clutch, however, was longer in profile and necessitated moving the engine back three centimetres (1.18 in) in the chassis. This, coupled with a total weight increase of 30 kg (66 lb) dictated further revisions to the suspension and an increase in rear tyre pressures from 2.4 to 3 bar (42 lb) which further accentuated the Turbo's somewhat hard ride characteristics.

The Turbo 3.3 is easily distinguished by the

Increasing the engine capacity to 3.3 litres raised the power output, but a real bonus comes from the intercooler unit atop the motor, which reduces the temperature of the charged air thus improving efficiency

Dry sump lubrication confuses many people who are not familiar with Porsches, so the vehicle identification plates in the engine bay include precise instructions on how to check the oil level. Other information includes valve clearances and the firing order (which most owners prefer to leave to qualified mechanics)

new, squared-off rear spoiler which is higher and larger with an upturned rubber surround carrying round the corners. Set into this 'wing' on the engine cover is a large grille which serves the air conditioning exchanger, the engine's intercooler and cooling fan.

If the 3-litre Turbo had deserved superlatives, the 3.3 was still more impressive. Importantly the more powerful engine, and the improved clutch, enabled the driver to spin the back wheels quite easily if he wanted to drive in that fashion, and the acceleration figures were greatly improved. From standstill to 60 mph now occupied a mere 5.3 seconds, with 100 mph coming up in 12.3 seconds, and according to *Motor* it was the fastest accelerating production car ever to pass through their

Careful space planning allowed the designers to fit an 80 litre fuel tank, but this necessitated using a Space-saver spare wheel. This has a collapsible sidewall, and the standard kit includes an electric air pump which plugs into the cigar lighter

hands—faster even than an AC Cobra or a Ferrari Daytona, though the Ferrari was quicker on maximum speed. With a genuine top speed of 160.1 mph, coupled with fuel consumption of the order of 15 to 20 miles per gallon (*Motor*'s overall figure including performance testing was 15.9 mpg) the Turbo offered a superb blend of performance, longevity and operating economy.

For a really fast journey on Europe's highways the Turbo is an obvious choice. It offers a completely effortless 130 mph given half a chance, more still if the driver is prepared to throw discretion to the winds so far as the law is concerned, and is easily able to pack more than 100 miles into every hour on motorways. On A-roads it is equally spectacular, treating slow-moving knots of traffic with disdain. Only on narrow, twisting roads would the Turbo be hard put to show its real potential, and I imagine that a couple of laps of the Nürburgring, or half an hour on Porsche's Weissach test track, could be

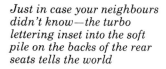

Just in case your neighbours didn't know—the turbo lettering inset into the soft pile on the backs of the rear seats tells the world

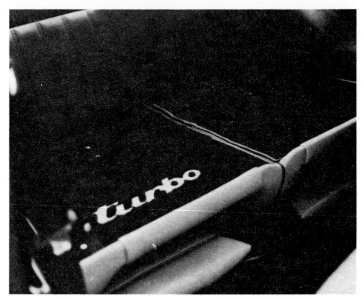

exhausting and sweaty experiences. Chassis engineer John Wheeler commented as much, saying that these exercises in the 928 S at similar speeds would be far more relaxing. But then of course, the 928 was designed a decade later with equal weight distribution, power steering, better ventilation, and still with 300 horsepower in 'S' form . . . that's progress.

Measured against the 928 S the Turbo is an anachronism, maybe, but it has a special place in the annals of car design.

The fascia is well equipped, with the tachometer dominating the speedometer and other instruments. A turbo boost gauge is set into the tachometer's face. EEC regulations requiring dual marking of the speedometer with mph and km/h spoiled the appearance of the matching instrument

Chapter 7
The specials

If one team should be singled out for mention in connection with Porsche's racing activities it is that run by the Cologne brothers Erwin and Manfred Kremer. Erwin, the elder brother and no mean driver himself on the tracks, has as a customer of Porsche's Sport Department run teams to capture a major title in every year since 1968 including three European championships in the GT class, seven Porsche Cups (the trophy awarded annually by the factory to the most successful customer entrant), culminating in outright victory at Le Mans in 1979 with a Kremer modified 935 driven by Klaus Ludwig and the American Whittington brothers, Bill and Don.

The company's title, Porsche Kremer Racing, suggests a high degree of loyalty to the Stuttgart firm's products, though racing is just the showcase for the Kremer brothers' real business of modifying street cars for customers who want faster, flashier or simply more expensive Porsches. A complete range of engine and body modifications is offered by the Kremers, tuned 911 SC engines hotted up from 204 to 225 horsepower, 3.3-litre 911s with similar power, and in the Turbo range conversions up to the order of 360 horsepower . . . all street legal and approved by the strict German licensing authorities.

The ultimate Kremer Porsche is the 'Group 5 Street R' version which closely resembles the K3

racing car. Ekkehard Zimmerman is the name of the man who has been building fibreglass body parts for the Kremers for ten years or more, and the most striking aspect of the 'R' is the entirely new, wrap-round frontal styling which incorporates the headlamps low down in the nose, just as on the racing cars. The front wings too are made out of fibreglass with hot air extractor slots on top. The oil cooler is situated in the nose of the car, just like the racing cars. The rear wheel arches, engine cover and tail panels are modified and include air inlets ahead of the wheels for brake cooling, and extractors aft, while the so-called 'whale tail' is also extended.

The b + b Targa version of the Turbo is something that the Porsche factory has never offered. Strengthening in the chassis adds weight to the car though the performance is virtually unaffected

99

Two of the Kremer brothers' K3 racing cars flank the ultimate roadgoing Turbo, the Kremer Group 5 Street model which has replica body panels. Improved aerodynamics raise the top speed to 174 mph without any engine modifications

Wider wheels, 8 in rims at the front and 9 in rear (or 9 in and 11 in if you want) carry extra-wide Pirelli P7 tyre equipment, which is well covered by the tailor-made bodywork.

The total effect is quite remarkable, especially if a special paint scheme has been applied, and a man owning a Porsche-Kremer Group 5 Street car

would indeed be king! Kremer will modify the
standard engine to 360 bhp if required, but as part
of this basic kit he instals a turbo boost control
knob between the seats enabling the driver to
increase the pressure from 0.8 bar (11.6 lb) to 1.2
bar (17.4 lb) just in case it became necessary to
dispose of a cheeky Ferrari Boxer on the way.

b + b went further still with this Targa Turbo. Take note of the doors and rear wings as well as the wheels (with rotation direction arrows!)

Kremer's aerodynamics certainly are an improvement, though drag figures aren't available, as evidenced by a *Sport Auto* test indicating that the top speed (with standard 0.8 bar boost) was increased by 20 km/h (12 mph) to 280 km/h— 174 mph. The cost of this (and if you need to ask you can't afford it!) is between DM 25,000 and DM 28,000 according to specification, in the region of £6000.

Pristine Porsche's handicraft puts 'racing' style wings onto 911 Turbos. No expense is spared

A Californian 911 Turbo Targa with those special front wings. There's nothing Pristine Porsche cannot do

Another German with a reputation for transformation is Rainer Buchmann from Frankfurt, whose b+b Exclusive company does for Porsches and other makes what Wood & Pickett did for the Mini. Going where Porsche chose not to tread, Buchmann produced a Targa version of the Turbo, and met the torsional stiffness problem head-on by reinforcing the floorpan and the doors. This added around 300 lb to the car's weight, but b+b customers cared little about that; all they wanted was a 911 Turbo Targa, something the factory wouldn't offer. Buchmann's bill for a full luxury conversion with suede seats, personalised interior and the ultimate in hi-fi could double the price of the Turbo, but for that sort of money he would include 928-style pop-up headlamps, gold leather, a radio-telephone, a cocktail bar and pretty well anything the customer wanted.

Over in America the tuning and reshaping industry has been interested in Porsche for many years, especially in California—not surprisingly, since traditionally half the Porsches made are exported to the States and half of those are sold in California. The climate is superb, making Targas a very popular type, so naturally enough someone had to follow in b+b wheeltracks with a Targa Turbo. Undoubtedly Dick Thorpe, proprietor of The Pristine Porsche speciality shop near Los Angeles was influenced by Buchman's work, right down to the exposed, upward-looking 928 pods.

Rivals Rick Norris and Neal Rayburn, proprietors of Rick's Porsche Service also in Los Angeles, make a very similar product with dropaway front fenders (wheel arches), the main difference being that the headlamps are enclosed, 924-style. Norris and Rayburn specialise in engine work, and one of their offerings is water injection direct into the manifold on a 3-litre Turbo which allows them to raise the boost to 0.9 bar without complications. According to *Car & Driver* the 911 shape is transformed by these sloping front fenders, allowing much better nearground visibility and making the car feel more spacious; not least, the aerodynamics are improved and the top speed is theoretically higher.

The factory itself, of course, offers a full range of engine conversions through its Sport Department, including anything from mild tuning on a 924 Turbo or a 911 SC up to a full replica of the Safari car for rally customers (this work costing

Dick Thorpe's Pristine Porsche speciality shop in California works to a high standard—the front fenders seem to point the way to the future. Here the treatment is subtle

around DM 90,000 on a car provided). Officially all development work on rear-engined models for competitions ceased in 1980, by which time all the Group 4 and Group 5 cars had been built, so that today the Sport Department is mainly concerned with customer work on the 924 Carrera family. Even so, factory conversions on the 911 Turbo are available.

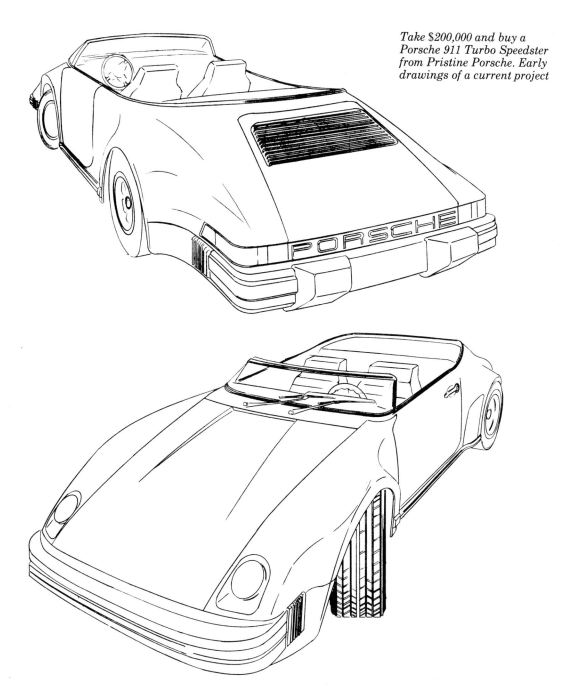

Take $200,000 and buy a Porsche 911 Turbo Speedster from Pristine Porsche. Early drawings of a current project

Chapter 8
What the road testers said

Like theatre reviews, car road test reports are not always a true reflection of the public reception awaiting a new creation. If they were, some types of car familiar on our roads just wouldn't be with us today. Price, equipment, availability and servicing all have a bearing on the success or otherwise but having said that, the opinion of journalists does have a distinct influence; maybe it's true that 100 kind words from a motoring writer can be worth 1000 words of copy in an advertisement. Generally weaned on bread-and-butter cars, most journalists can be relied upon to eulogise over a high performance machine coming from a reputable manufacturer. We have to turn to some of the world's serious motor journals for the critical analyses which make or mar the newborn's chances in the world.

Few cars have been heralded so rapturously as the Porsche 911 Turbo and the car has stood the test of time. Harold 'Dev' Dvoretsky, writing for the Australian journal *Modern Motor* stated in January 1975: 'The Porsche Turbo has finally thrown the German company into direct competition with the Italian exotics. Instead of competing against cheap models in the sporty car line-up such as Ferrari Dinos and Lamborghini

Urracos, Porsche now lines up against the top-of-the-line models—Berlinetta Boxer (what's 7000 dollars between exotics?), Espada, and the new Aston Martin Lagonda.'

Roger Bell, then editor of *Motor*, commented after his first test run: 'It's the combination of peace and power that makes this incredible machine unique in my experience. We've tested he-man cars before that were as quick as the Porsche (the Holman-Moody tuned 7-litre Cobra and the Ford GT40 stand out in my memory) but they were brutal, frenzied, writhing machines that bombarded practically all your senses with their aggressiveness and noise.

Porsche Cars' Great Britain demonstrator in an unglamorous pose, but showing off the 300 horsepower power plant

109

*Side view of the Porsche
Turbo 3.3 in its latest form
with twin exhaust tailpipes,
this system being slightly
more efficient. The indicator
repeaters on the side of the
wings identify the 1981
models*

'What makes the Turbo so different is that it hurls you forward with similar ferocity but in an uncannily quiet and effortless way. To be shoved so hard in the back that you *need* high-back seats to keep your head on, yet neither to feel nor hear anything more than a muffled hum, is a very odd sensation indeed in a car. It's rather like sitting up front in a VC10 jet on take-off when you're forced into the seat by some mysterious and remote power.

'To experience this sort of acceleration in a car without the customary noise is certainly very deceptive. Some people may even call it deceitful because in a curious way it cheats you out of some of the excitement that might be expected of a high-performance car that we understand will cost £14,000 when deliveries start next year.

'Up to 3,000 rpm the performance is nothing special—quick, but not sensational ... once you're doing 3,500 rpm or thereabouts the engine responds instantly to the throttle. Just a slight touch will send the car surging forth.' In on-off conditions though, Bell commented that the turbocharger had time to slow down and lead to some delay in answering the throttle, "but it's all quite simple once you've programmed your right foot to do everything a couple of seconds earlier than normal.' This report noted that the car was entirely tractable in London's traffic, and commented on the low exhaust noise which was, characteristically, muffled by the turbo.

In the spring of 1975 journalists were offered the chance to drive out from the Geneva Show, though full road tests were to come later ... the reason for this was clear when the writers were asked not to undertake any fierce standing starts on account of the gearbox not being the production type. Ray Hutton, editor of *Autocar*, decided that 'it is scarcely typical of the £15,000

club to which it belongs. It doesn't shout "expensive", and you need to be an ardent 911 enthusiast to distinguish it from the Carrera, which is nearly £5,000 cheaper.

'Neither does it spell racing-type "performance", we reflected, as we ambled through the busy streets of Geneva and the Turbo's engine ticked over quietly and unobtrusively in the traffic jams. There was no fluffing, no temperature or temperament problems. Nothing to indicate what was to come.

'We headed out of the city towards the motorway and thence to the mountains. That first

Some engine! A mass of machinery which only just fits the engine bay of the Turbo 3.3, a space originally designed for a 130 horsepower 2-litre engine. The turbocharger (on the left of the aluminised silencer box) is normally hidden from view

113

All the stages of construction are by hand, all of Porsche's production line workers being craftsmen. The chassis is assembled on moving jigs

burst of acceleration from a cruising 50 mph on to the clear ribbon of concrete road ahead summed up the Porsche Turbo for both of us. It wasn't a kick in the back, more the action of a heavy yet gentle giant hand pushing us forward as a child might a model car. The engine note, still quiet, rose only slightly and was unbroken by misfires or hesitation. There was no sudden leap forward as with most turbocharged cars. Initially the tail dipped slightly and then, just perceptibly, one could detect the under-bumper air dam and the big rear spoiler balancing out the car as it entered the higher speed regime; something neither of us had experienced in quite this way in a road car: 200 kph, 220, 250 . . . 155 mph. the Turbo seemed

only then to be getting into its stride; it was still accelerating strongly'.

American journalist Pete Lyons, writing for *Autosport*, had mixed feelings about the Turbo after driving it at the Hockenheim race circuit in Germany. He found it immensely fast and quite addictive, but a real handful on a race track in admittedly inexperienced hands. 'When trying to drive carefully, somewhat below what seemed to be the limit, it seemed extraordinarily difficult to predict what the car was going to do; besides that, the very quick acceleration would almost always sling me around to the exit faster and wider than I expected. By the end of the corner I was simply along for the ride, foot trying not to let up too

Engines are assembled on a slow-moving line, and each one is tested on a dynomometer before installation into the chassis

115

The Turbo is now taking shape. The body is made entirely of galvanised steel and carries a 7-year warranty against corrosion

much on the power but my hands a frantic scramble all over the steering wheel; I was only rarely *with* the car. I was usually a step or two or three behind. Should I let up on the power the tail would come around viciously. Should I keep the brakes dragging too late while turning in, again the back would carry on towards the outside. During several hard, untidy laps I managed to not quite spin the car, but twice I was well off on the wide grassy inside verge with my arms crossed and my foot on the clutch wondering how in hell I had managed *that*!

'That it was too much for me personally to handle properly is no reflection on the car itself, I think. This is a car that demands, clearly, an unusual degree of responsibility of its master; this is finally a matter for him alone to appreciate. That said, treated as a very powerful, nimble, ultra responsive road car, it's a compellingly magnificent one.'

The author, then editor of *Motoring News* agreed with Lyons about the handling calling for respect. 'Up to the danger mark, which is far quicker than you could drive on most public roads, there is mild understeer, and the limiting factor on our one-way track was taking care not to apply too much throttle coming out of fast bends in case the turbocharger should come in so hard as to affect the car's balance. To say that we were mindful of the possibilities is an understatement! On a slower handling course we pushed the car a little harder, finding that when breakaway point is reached eventually the rear end can lose adhesion quite suddenly and call for rapid action on the steering wheel. We did not drive the Turbo in the rain but we believe that it would have demanded considerable respect.' Certainly though the performance was all that had been expected, *Motoring News* describing the

Down the line for trimming and glazing. By now each car is being finished to a particular customer's order, with its own identification

*Now the body is fully
trimmed, waiting for the
engine and suspension units
to be offered up*

Turbo as 'a ground-hugging projectile' that
accelerated 'as though released from a giant
catapult.'

The car's reception in the United States was to
be all-important to the Porsche company, and the
Turbo was put on the road to success by excellent
reviews in the two magazines that matter most,
Road & Track and *Car & Driver*. Patrick Bedard,
writing for *C & D* opened: 'It's not magic—just
superior engineering. The Turbo Carrera's supercharging system is exactly what you'd expect of
Porsche: complex, sophisticated and extremely
effective. At low speeds the only difference a
driver would notice between the normally-

aspirated 2.7-litre 911 and the 3.0-litre Turbo is a very slight lag in the Turbo's throttle response. The Turbo's power seems to double in the 500 rpm span between 2,700 and 3,200, accompanied by a hissing roar from the tailpipe as the volume of exhaust gases increases in proportion to the power. Under full boost, the Turbo has the feel of a much larger engine.'

And in *R & T* Joe Rusz reported: 'Porsche's heavy artillery for '76 is the Turbo Carrera, a dazzlingly fast road car that shares a common heritage with Porsche racing cars of the last few seasons. Its body and suspension are spinoffs from the Group 4 RSR, while its engine is a detuned

The body is lowered onto the engine and running gear, and now the completed car is nearly ready for a searching road test before being consigned for shipment

version of the Group 5 racing Turbo powerplant. Yet in spite of a heavy infusion of racing blood, the Turbo Carrera is easily the fastest and most civilised 911 ever built. Top speed is a respectable 155 mph, while 0–60 mph acceleration times are in the 5- to 6-second bracket. Unfortunately, the Turbo's top speed is commensurate with its price. Both are high, meaning that the 400 or so lucky 1976 US buyers will have to pay about 26,000 dollars for their very own Turbo.

'The Turbo is the epitome of Porsches. Fast, yes, but driveable too. Under normal conditions it's like any other late model 911, but mash the throttle and things start to happen. The response is not instantaneous, especially at low speeds, but it is noticeable and as the revs build so does the engine output. Yet through it all the engine remains remarkably quiet. One is not aware that in very little time he is travelling at over 150 mph, as I discovered on TRC's banked test track. Handling is noticeably improved and the 911's legendary oversteer is more subdued than before.

'Driver comfort in the Turbo is exceptional, but then this is a luxury GT. Using the new self-regulating heater or the air conditioner, one can conceivably dial in a desirable temperature, then relax and listen to the stereo as the miles sweep by.'

Denis Jenkinson, Continental editor of *Motor Sport*, has had a love affair with Porsches since his ownership of a 356 which features large in an Osprey companion book. His reaction in 1977 to the famous Porsche Turbo Martini show car was interesting. 'I never thought the day would come when Ferraris, Maseratis, Lamborghinis and similar exotica would pale into insignificance in my book of motoring, but that day came with the Porsche Turbo. If you get the impression that I was really turned on by the Porsche, you are

absolutely correct; in fact, the last time a fast car impressed me as much was the Ford GT40.

'As it stood there on the show stand the price was £21,162 and when I went to collect it from Isleworth, after it had been run-in, I found it hard to accept that a Porsche could be worth over £20,000. However, when I returned it a week later I had changed my mind completely, convinced that Porsche were offering £20,000 worth of performance, engineering, quality and above all else, integrity in all things, which was most heart-warming in these days of the spurious, the artificial, the shoddy and the plain nasty.

Now 'the Turbo' has a young rival—the 924 Turbo which offers high road performance from a 2-litre, four-cylinder engine . . . at about half the cost

The 924 Turbo engine (Type 931) which develops 177 horsepower, and gives the 143 mph performance. The cross-bracing strut is a competitions part

'When talking to Porsche factory people, or for that matter their agents, you are very conscious that they all believe in Porsche implicitly, as well they might, and that Dr. Ferry Porsche, and his illustrious father before him, are revered by one and all. Not in the rather mystical way that Enzo Ferrari is revered by Ferrari owners, or Ettore Bugatti was in his day, but in a solid and sound engineering sense, an admiration for a way of doing things and a way of thinking.'

And of the car itself: 'An unsupercharged 3-litre Porsche engine has pretty impressive acceleration, but when the boost comes in it is electrifying. There is no sudden surge of power or kick in the back, merely an ever-increasing pressure on the back of the seat and all without increase in noise level, or any feeling of fuss or strain. The smoothness and quietness is uncanny and you appreciate why the rev-counter is the most prominent instrument; without it you would have no idea of what speed the engine was turning at ... the straight-line performance of this Porsche-turbo is almost more than one is prepared to unleash on the open road; indeed, I used all its acceleration in 1st, 2nd and 3rd gears, reaching 117 mph in 3rd at 6,000 rpm and full boost, and felt that the continuing acceleration in 4th gear from that point was almost more than I wanted to cope with, and that is the first car that has given me that feeling on the road.'

Jenks concluded his report: 'These are quality standards to which Porsche engineering work when building what must be the ultimate motor car. The sports car is not dead, it's alive and well and being built in Stuttgart.'

Bigger and better

In order to qualify as a supercar, the model in question has to deliver the goods—that's of paramount importance. Almost any Ferrari qualifies automatically, Maseratis used to (but have to work harder these days to maintain the reputation), and in our opinion the Turbo put Porsche into the top league for the first time. It's all tied up with mystique and whilst the 911 was forever admired by Porsche enthusiasts, the Turbo was the first derivative to enthral them.

For years, in the 1950s and 1960s, Porsche had been pitching for class wins with up-to-2-litre cars on the race tracks; the 3-litre 908 started winning races—and championships—more regularly than any predecessor, but the fabulous 917 really took Porsche to the top of the league. It was all about power and spectacle, and the flat-12 racing car created a legend that needed emulating in the production car range. The Carrera 2.7/3.0 got close, but the Turbo finally made the grade.

If the 3-litre Turbo finally established Porsche in the supercar league, how much better the 3.3?

This was summed up succinctly by *Road and Track* thus: 'Outrageous, simply outrageous. That's the reaction of every staff member who drove the 1978 version of the Porsche Turbo. How else can we describe a car with this much acceleration and unrestrained performance? On those all too rare occasions when we have a car like this to road test and report on, it's much too easy to talk about exhilaration and excitement . . . that word, outrageous, is the one we find most fitting in describing the Turbo's acceleration as it sped from rest to 60 mph in 5.0 seconds! It went to 30 mph in less than 2.0 seconds. One hundred mph in 11.9 seconds. The Turbo burst through the standing-start quarter-mile test in 13.7 seconds at a speed of 106.5 mph. As numbers on a page, these are interesting, but being in the car while all this is happening is incredible: the engine gets revved to 4,000 rpm, the left foot steps off the clutch, the super-wide-P7 rear tyres chirp and hop a couple of times but don't really spin, and you're off and being pushed down the pavement in a big hurry. And noise to go with it? Nope, not much. The turbocharger hides most of the traditional Porsche exhaust growl and because it's all happening out back, there isn't the thundering noise level associated with the Sixties' supercars that could perform in this manner.

'On the road the Turbo can be a frustrating car to drive, because all that performance is there for the asking but there are few opportunities to use it. Using more than 3,000 rpm and about quarter-throttle position simply isn't necessary. Nor legal. As one staffer noted, "if I owned this car, I'd either have ulcers from frustration or no driver's license!"

'The turbocharger still makes this Porsche's performance peaky but less so than with the earlier models. You start to feel the boost around 3,000 rpm and then at 3,600–3,800 rpm all hell breaks loose from there to the redline. What fun!

'In driving the Turbo around southern California between rain-storms and during the track testing, the Pirelli P7 tyres gave impressive ride comfort and control. However, the tread is noisy and these tyres don't take sharp inputs such as highway lane bumps well, thumping badly and loudly. In getting on and off the throttle during spirited cornering to test the tyres' transient response, we found the P7s much more forgiving than the CN36s and we also attribute a portion of the Turbo's excellent braking performance to the P7s.'

Despite the longer wheelbase, and the development carried out to handling, *R & T* still found the Turbo a handful when pressed to the limit. 'We found that expected transition from under- to over-steer and vice versa is always there and ready to catch the unwary driver who backs off the throttle in a tight corner or applies a heavy foot to the throttle and brings on the boost. It was a question of keeping the engine off the boost by using a higher gear and light throttle; otherwise

127

the turbocharger boost would come on with a rush and change the handling characteristics dramatically.'

The last word in press comment comes from *Motor* magazine, the only British journal to have conducted a full test on the Turbo 3.3. The schedule included a visit to VW's test track at Ehra-Lessein north of Wolfsburg, the only closed circuit in northern Europe where the Turbo's 160 mph top speed could be checked (and interestingly, the maximum speed runs clocked 158.1 mph in one direction and 162.1 mph in the other, for an average of 160.1 mph). *Motor*'s staff covered over 900 miles in under 18 hours in a round-the-clock dash to Germany, and were astonished to average 17.5 miles per gallon overall despite running the car at close to maximum speed for long stretches.

Motor's road test report published in May 1979 showed almost undiluted enthusiasm from beginning to end, referring to the Turbo as 'the quickest production car we (and as far as we know, anyone else) have ever tested.'

The Turbo was given the top rating of five stars (excellent) for performance, handling, braking, finish and equipment—most road test cars are lucky to get a single five-star rating!—and four stars (good) for transmission, ride comfort, 'at the wheel', visibility and instruments. Three star ratings (average) were accorded to economy, accommodation, heating and noise level, while two stars (poor) were awarded to ventilation.

Motor's summary read thus: 'We said of the 3-litre Turbo that few, if any, cars have impressed us so much. That's a difficult act to follow, but the 3.3-litre version is an even better car which fully lives up to Porsche's claim that it offers "racing performance with saloon car comfort."

'Its acceleration is simply breathtaking, and the maximum speed is very high, but the same may be said for a number of "supercars". Likewise, its astonishing roadholding and its powerful brakes are matched by a select few of the world's best motor cars, though none has the same astonishingly sensitive feel.

'The real achievement of the Turbo is its supreme practicability. It is as much at home dawdling along the High Street as it is flat out on the *autobahn*. It can be treated like an ordinary everyday car, and indeed, there is nothing on the market at *any* price which has a longer interval between recommended services. In our opinion it is probably the best example of precision engineering on four wheels.'

A look at the performance figures, the most authentic available on a European specification car, would be an interesting conclusion.

Acceleration from rest

mph	sec	mph	sec
0–30	2.2	0–80	7.8
0–40	2.7	0–90	10.3
0–50	3.7	0–100	12.3
0–60	5.3	0–110	15.0
0–70	6.4	0–120	19.1

Standing quarter-mile: 13.4 sec (104 mph). Standing kilometre, 22.9 sec. (124 mph).

Acceleration in top

mph	sec	mph	sec
20–40	9.8	70–90	5.7
30–50	9.6	80–100	6.1
40–60	9.1	90–110	7.3
50–70	7.2	100–120	8.7
60–80	6.0		

Specifications

	1975 to 1977	1977 on
Engine	*Turbo 3.0*	*Turbo 3.3*
Cylinders	Six	Six
Bore	95 mm (3.74 in)	97 mm (3.82 in)
Stroke	70.4 mm (2.77 in)	74.4 mm (2.93 in)
Capacity	2993 cc (182.64 cu. in)	3299 cc (201.3 cu. in)
Compression ratio	6.5:1	7:1
Maximum power (DIN)	260 @ 5500 rpm	300 @ 5500 rpm
Maximum torque (DIN)	254 lb. ft @ 4000 rpm	304 lb. ft @ 4000 rpm
Output per litre (DIN)	87 bhp	91 bhp
Intercooler	No	Yes
Fuel octane rating	96	98

Engine design

Layout	Air-cooled, six-cylinder, four-stroke, horizontally opposed. Dry sump lubrication.
Crankcase	Light alloy
Cylinders	Light alloy
Valve position	One inlet, one exhaust; inverted V-pattern
Valve operation	Single overhead camshaft for each bank, chain driven
Fuel supply	Twin electric pumps
Crankshaft	Forged steel, in eight main bearings
Fuel injection	Bosch K-Jetronic continuous injection system (CIS), with KKK turbocharger.
Electrical system	Capacitor discharge, contactless

Transmission

Clutch	Single dry plate, 240 mm diameter (9.6 in)
Manual gearbox	Four forward speeds, with Porsche synchromesh
Final drive	Spiral bevel differential, with limited slip option
Ratio	9:38 (4.222:1)

Chassis, suspension

Front suspension	Independent, with wishbones and MacPherson struts
Rear suspension	Torsion bars, telescopic shock absorbers, with independent semi-trailing arms layout
Anti-roll bars	Front and rear

Brakes	Front, 284 mm Ventilated Rear, 290 mm Ventilated	Front, 304 mm Ventilated/cross-drilled Rear, 309 mm Ventilated/cross-drilled
Servo	No	Yes
Wheels	Light alloy, forged 7J × 15 front (until 1976) 8J × 15 rear (until 1976)	Light alloy, forged 7J × 16 front (from 1976) 8J × 16 rear (from 1976)
Steering	Rack and pinion	Rack and pinion.
Fuel tank capacity	80 litres (17.6 Imp. gal)	

Dimensions

Wheelbase	2272 mm (89.45 in)	2272 mm (89.45 in)
Track, front	1438 mm (56.61 in)	1432 mm (56.38 in)
Track, rear	1511 mm (59.49 in)	1501 mm (59.09 in)
Length	4291 mm (168.94 in)	4291 mm (168.94 in)
Width	1775 mm (69.88 in)	1775 mm (69.88 in)
Height	1310 mm (51.57 in)	1310 mm (51.57 in)
Weight	1195 kg (2635 lb)	1300 kg (2866 lb)*

*Weights according to optional equipment fitted.

Production schedules

	Chassis numbers	total in year
1975 model year (to August 1975)		
'Rest of the world'	930.570.0011 to 930.570.0284	274
USA	None	
Japan	None	
1976 model year (to August 1976)		
'Rest of the world'	930.670.0011 to 930.670.0664	654
USA	930.680.0011 to 930.680.0530	530
Japan	Included in 'world' series	(28)
RSR 934 Group 4	930.670.0151 to 930.670.0180	30
1977 model year (to August 1977)		
'Rest of world'	930.770.0011 to 930.770.0996	986
USA	930.780.0011 to 930.780.0727	717
Japan	Included in 'world' series	(49)
RSR 934 Group 4	930.770.0951 to 930.770.0960	10
935 Group 5	930.770.0901 to 930.770.0913	13
1978 model year (to August 1978)		
'Rest of world'	930.870.0011 to 930.870.0735	725
USA	930.880.0011 to 930.880.0461	451
Japan	930.870.9511 to 930.870.9561	50
RSR 935 Group 5	930.890.0001 to 930.890.0025	25
1979 model year (to August 1979)		
'Rest of world'	930.970.0011 to 930.970.0820	809
USA	930.980.0011 to 930.980.0816	806
Japan	930.970.9511 to 930.970.9532	22
RSR 935 Group 5	930.990.0001 to 930.990.0032	32
1980 model year (to August 1980)		
'Rest of world'	93A.007.0011 to 93A.007.0840	830
USA (continue 1979 series)	930.980.0817 to 930.980.1200	384
Japan	Included in 'world' series	(63)
Total:		7348

Acknowledgements

It would be fitting to thank the Porsche company for making the cars which made this book possible. Also Ian Geekie for the production data, John Wheeler for background information, and Graham Poulter Associates Ltd for the front cover photograph.

Further grateful thanks must be extended to all those named and nameless people (ignorance, rather than intent) who also supplied the illustrations. Alphabetically; b + b Exclusive, Rob de la Rive Box, Mirco Decet, Martin Holmes, Erwin Kremer, LAT, Lepp and Associates, Jean-Francois Marchet, Herbert Meinzer, Rich McCormack of The Newport Press, Porsche Werkfoto, Pristine Porsche, Clive Sherwood, Jerry Sloniger and Van Hallam.

Index

A

AC Cobra **96, 109**
Alfa Romeo T33 **18**
Aston Martin Lagonda **109**
Autocar **7, 84, 85, 112**
Autosport **115**

B

b + b Exclusive **44, 104**
Bedard, Patrick **120**
Bell, Roger **102, 109**
Bentley 4½ **6**
Berger, Wolfgang **23, 51**
Bilstein **27, 43**
BMW **61**
BMW 2002 Turbo **33**
Bondurant, Bob **7**
Bosch **27, 40, 51, 63**
Buchi, Alfred **12**
Buchmann, Rainer **104**
Bugatti, Ettore **124**

C

California **127**
Can-Am **13, 17, 23**
Car & Driver **7, 105, 120**
Chevrolet Corvette **25**
Cologne **98**

D

Daytona 24-Hours **18, 32**
De Tomaso Pantera **25**
Donohue, Mark **16, 17, 18**
Dunlop **55**

E

Earls Court **83**
Ehra-Lessein **128**

F

Ferrari **18, 122, 124, 125**
Ferrari Boxer **101, 109**
      Daytona **6, 25, 96**
Ferrari, Enzo **124**
FIA **13, 18**
Flegl, Helmuth **23**
Follmer, George **17, 52**
Ford GT40 **6, 75, 123**
Fuhrmann, Professor Dr.
  Ernst **7, 9, 23, 38, 83**

G

Garrett **19, 41**
Geneva Salon **33, 34, 73,**
  112, 113
Gregg, Peter **18, 32**
Gulf-Mirage **18**

H

Haywood, Hurley **18, 32**
Hezemans, Toine **52**
Hockenheim **15, 62, 115**
Holman-Moody **109**
Horsman, John **75**
Hutchinson, Jeff **73**
Hutton, Ray **112**

I

Ickx, Jacky **62**
Indianapolis **13**

J

Jaguar D type **6**
Jantke, Manfred **73**
Jenkinson, Denis **73, 122,**
  125

K

KKK **19, 40**
Kremer, Erwin **62, 98, 101**
     Manfred **98**

L

Lamborghini **122**
Lamborghini Urraco **109**
Lancia **62**
Lausanne **73**
Le Mans **21, 22, 40, 51, 52,**
  61, 62, 98
London **73**
Los Angeles **105**
Ludwig, Klaus **98**
Lyons, Pete **115, 118**

M

Martini **83, 122**
Maserati **122, 125**
Matra **18, 22**
McLaren **17**
Meyer-Drake **13**
Mezger, Hans **14, 24**
Mini **104**
MIRA **75**
Monza **22**
Motor **7, 94, 96, 109, 128**
Motoring News **118**
Motor Sport **122**
Muller, Herbert **18**

Munich **61**

N
Nikasil **18, 38, 89**
Norisring **62**
Norris, Rick **105**
Nürburgring **96**

O
Oliver, Jack **73**

P
Paris Show **8, 33, 73**
Penske, Roger **17**
Pirelli **38, 50, 80, 82, 85, 100, 127**
Porsche Cup **98**
Porsche, Dr. Ferry **23, 124**
Porsche, Professor **12, 80**
Porsche Sport Department **98, 105, 106**
Porsche Carrera 6 **19**
  356 Carrera **23**
  908 **126**
  911 **8, 9, 18, 21, 24, 25, 26, 27, 30, 33, 38, 40, 48, 50, 52, 83, 85, 97, 98, 105, 113, 121, 126**
  917 **13, 14, 17, 27, 49**
  924 **7, 62, 105, 106**
  928 **38, 97, 105**
Pristine Porsche **105**

R
Rayburn, Neal **105**
Reiter **24**
Ricard **21**
Rick's Porsche Service **105**
Road & Track **120, 121, 126, 127**
Rusz, Joe **121**

S
Safari **105**
Schaeffer, Valentine **14**
Siffert, Jo **13**
Silverstone **61**
Singer, Norbert **24, 32, 51, 57**
Sport Auto **102**
Stuttgart **12, 13, 98, 125**

T
Talladega **18**
Targa Florio **18**
Thorpe, Dick **105**
Thyssen **81**

V
VC10 **112**
Volkswagen **12, 128**
Volkswagen Beetle **80**

W
Weissach **7, 15, 23, 50, 80, 96**
Wheeler, John **48, 97**
Whittington, Bill **98**
  Don **98**
Windsor, Peter **84**
Wolfsburg **128**
Wood & Pickett **104**

Z
Zimmermann, Ekkehard **99**
Zuffenhausen **6, 51**